Life's a
Bitch!

Life's a Bitch!

A Canine Commentary on Human Affairs

by

Dido

Assisted by
CHAPMAN PINCHER

SWAN·HILL
PRESS

Copyright © 1996 Chapman Pincher
First published in the UK in 1996
by Swan Hill Press, an imprint of Airlife Publishing Ltd

British Library Cataloguing in Publication Data
A catalogue record for this book
is available from the British Library

ISBN 1 85310 829 4

Typeset by Hewer Text Composition Services, Edinburgh
Printed in England by Livesey Ltd, Shrewsbury

Swan Hill Press
an imprint of Airlife Publishing Ltd
101 Longden Road, Shrewsbury SY3 9EB, England

Contents

Foreword

by Chapman Pincher

Writers of science fiction have often wondered how a visitor from Mars, surveying the earthly scene with a different kind of mind, might view the customs, beliefs and general behaviour of the human species. My remarkable chocolate Labrador, Dido, believes that there is no need to wait for such an unlikely event because a different creature with such a capability already exists on earth in the shape of herself. Dido lays claim to a unique brand of objectivity that she calls 'dogjectivity' – a capacity incorporating the advantages of the exceptional intimacy of the dog–man relationship which permits a degree of understanding and appreciation of human affairs that would be denied to any Martian.

Though it has long been suspected, it has only recently been proved by scientific study that dogs dream as regularly and vividly as we do. So there seems to be no reason to doubt Dido's claim that she also fantasises as we do, imagining herself in all manner of intriguing situations. As an established author, with further literary ambitions, she has chosen the medium of fantasy as the chief means of recording her sometimes caustic commentary on the human scene. It may be no coincidence that Fantasy is Dido's second name for she was registered at the Kennel Club as Keneven Fantasy, Dido being the short name she was given for convenience.

As Dido's ghost-writer, responsible for translating her commentaries into English, I may be responsible for the odd misinterpretation but the basics are essentially hers. Flavouring her satirical stories with her earthy sense of humour, as she does, she can be accused of mixing fact with fantasy but, then, who doesn't?

Chapman Pincher
Kintbury, Berks.

Prodog

With admirable bluntness, the immortal Scottish bard, Doggie Burns, wrote:

> Oh wad some Pow'r the giftie gie ye,
> To see yoursels as doggies see ye!
> It wad frae mony a blunder free ye,
> And foolish notion.

It is with that service in mind that I present this collection of canine musings about the crazy caravan of capers, customs, beliefs and institutions which constitute human behaviour. Being of a different species, I can view this behaviour with a degree of objectivity and detachment denied to any human mind trammelled, as it must be, with tradition, prejudice and delusion. People abandon their pretences in the presence of their household dogs who see and hear everything as it really is. So, after eight years of head-shaking wonder, I feel well qualified to present my views on the human predicament.

When passing judgement on people, especially the high and mighty, it is unfair to abstract them from the environments in which they have to operate. So, to be fair with my criticism, I have put myself in human situations through the process of fantasy, when the mind can range freely and private feelings can be expressed uninhibited by excessive respect or fear of reprisal. Like a man who day-dreams while sucking at a pipe, I do the same while sucking at a marrowbone on the lawn, being lost in fantasy but awake enough not only to gnaw my bone but to move with my patch of sunshine when it moves.

It is a widespread belief in the human world that some of the greatest truths have been revealed to serious thinkers through fantasy, in which we all spend more time than we care to admit – yet another way in which we resemble one another. I suspect that in my meditations – of which I have kept a detailed diary record – secrets of human behaviour have been vouchsafed to me through this same process of revelation. When such a bone has been the medium of further insight into your quirks I bury what remains of it with special satisfaction.

I trust that those with whose names I have taken liberties will not take offence at being used in the efforts of a not-so-dumb animal to make more sense of the world in which she finds herself. Perhaps, in view of the intimate nature of some of my mental adventures, my bark should have been sealed but if, in the process of giving tongue, I have undermined a few human pretensions, punctured some pomposities and exposed a few hypocrisies I could not be more pleased. Besides, I need the money.

CHAPTER 1
Pawballer of the Year

It all began when I was carved in bronze by our famous village sculptor, Willie Newton, who specialises in horses but wanted to move upwards, socially, into dogs. Before beginning to model me in clay, from which the bronze casting would be made, he needed to watch me in motion in the garden. So, to make me move around with speed – and, it goes without saying, with grace – my Chap brought out the full-size football he had bought me for our garden games and punted it around the lawn. I was on to it in a flash, dribbling it past him with my paws into a corner, where I could pick it up with my mouth using an ingenious trick I had devised.

On the way, I overran the ball slightly and Willie spotted the perfect poise in which he wanted to freeze me in bronze for posterity – with my chest resting, momentarily, on the ball and all four legs in the air!

The moment Willie announced that he had seen enough to be inspired and began to manipulate his clay, the Chap lost interest which meant that I did too, for what self-respecting dog wants to play on her own? Besides, it was warm and sunny and time for my siesta. The Boss had kindly put my beanbag on the lawn and puffed it up in case my sculptor had wanted to model me sitting on it. So I stretched out on it in my favourite resting posture with my latest bone between my paws, hind legs splayed and the sun beating down on me. With the ball safely beside me – I like to keep my most treasured possessions within a paw's reach – I fell to day-dreaming in a way which gave new meaning to the current craze for 'fantasy football'.

In a bid to improve its image in the Premier League, that great team, Man United, had upgraded its name to Dog United. At the same time, the team manager had seen a picture of my sculpture in a national newspaper after it had been briefly exhibited at the Tate Gallery, alongside a dead sheep, and liked the look of my style, obvious ball control and competitive spirit. So when he decided that Cantona should be held back as substitute in a crucial home game with Newcastle United which could settle the Championship, he telephoned me and asked me to play in a striker role. Other canines may have been approached but, if so, they had lacked the courage or brass nerve, however you care to look at it. So I was the only dog in the squad – ten men and a dog. It's great having one man to play with for a full hour and a half. The prospect of ten was irresistible.

Before inviting me to play, the directors had studied the laws of the game and found there was nothing to bar me. The laws refer to eleven 'players' with nothing specifying 'men', which is why boys and women can play, so I qualified. I suppose this means that they could put an elephant in goal if they were so minded, since there is no limit on the size of the goalkeeper, but nobody had thought of that, though after reading it here they probably will now.

When I turned up for training at the Old Trafford ground it was pointed out that the laws of Association Football state that a player must wear colours, but I did that anyway, being chocolate all over and always wearing a wide, yellow collar. For other obvious reasons nobody was ever going to confuse me with anybody else on the pitch, but it was suggested that, for conformity's sake, I should wear a red jersey. With nothing on at all I might be mistaken for one of those streakers – human oddballs who can find no way of drawing attention to themselves other than running naked on to a field. In the end, we settled for a wide, red collar which I felt was enough for an opponent to grab at, considering the extent to which most footballers foul that way these days, as is revealed every time a match is televised. Also, I feel undressed without a collar and always fear that I might catch a cold. The collar had my name and the number seven on it, boldly in white, which I felt was a lucky omen because that was the number of pups in my one and only litter and each of those was a winner. Was it a portent? Could I produce seven goals in one session?

The question of boots was also raised but there is no rule insisting that a player should wear boots and some African sides play without them so, feeling that four boots would look ridiculous and would slow me up, we settled for bare paws. The only rule which raised any real difficulty for me was the one which forbids touching the ball with the hands but, as there is nothing in the book about paws, it was deemed that, legally, I was OK on that score as well. The manager would raise the matter before the match with the referee and convince him that, as any dog walks on four legs, the front paws must count as feet, which is what football is mainly about. And there is nothing in the rules requiring players to have only two. The only special warning I received was that I would be given a card to match my red collar and be sent off if I obeyed a call of nature, especially in the goal-mouth, something which a dog of my breeding and upbringing would never contemplate.

Frankly, I was rather disappointed by the training session, expecting to receive a lot of valuable advice about passing, dribbling and using my head, but it was not so much about tactics as about pleasing the fans. A lot of the time was spent instructing me in what to do if I scored, like punching the air, turning somersaults, strutting and generally dancing about like a dog on hot bricks.

As a Yorkshireman, the Chap disapproved of my playing for a Lancashire club, this business about the Wars of the Roses still rankling after five hundred years, which seems quite crazy to any dog. Furthermore, as he had lived most of his young life on the Durham border and regards himself as a bit of a Geordie, he instinctively favours Newcastle, commonly known as the Magpies because of their black-and-white striped shirts. Nevertheless, he agreed to drive me to the Old Trafford ground and watch from the bunker if that could be fixed, which it was, without much difficulty, as he is really my manager, among other things such as chauffeur, walker, groom, valet, ghost-writer and general adoguensis. He was, of course, also concerned to be on hand in case I should be stretchered off injured, being especially anxious that my writing capacity should not be affected as he has a pecuniary interest through our joint account for my royalties at Lloyds Bank. Once he knew that I was going to be on *Match of the Day*, he agreed with me that the risk of injury was worthwhile for the publicity. The team manager had been equally aware of that advantage and my appearance had been widely advertised. So a packed stadium was assured, especially as the Geordies were sending the maximum contingent of supporters.

I had never imagined that I would be the target of political incorrectness but, as I cantered out of the tunnel and on to the pitch, the Newcastle supporters started pelting me with bones, in the same way they used to throw bananas at some black players. They continued to do it whenever I got the ball, booing at the same time until parts of the field looked like a butcher's shop. I had not fully realised the extent to which the yob culture had invaded the game. No player should be barred or booed on grounds of race, creed, sex, colour or species. I was determined that I wouldn't take any nonsense but I would not make the mistake of giving any spectator a four-paw Cantona special. If it became too bad I would warn the referee that I intended to sue for damages for hurt feelings in the European Court of Canine Rights and he could announce it over the public address system. Anyway, if the yobs were hoping to distract me they failed because I ignored them as beneath canine contempt. I must admit, though, that some of the bones were very tempting, especially when the ball was at the other end of the field, and I made a mental note to take the best of them home in a doggie bag, if I could find one. Regrettably, all I could see on or around the pitch were toilet rolls which, in an expensive gesture, spectators kept throwing at both goalkeepers. I think the goalies had the same idea as me because they kept gathering up the toilet rolls, presumably for future use.

From the kick-off I was on to the ball right away and I didn't stop to pick daisies, not that there were any on the pitch. With so much practice at running rings around the Chap, I dictated the pace of the game with my speed and agility. There were roars of 'Handball!' and 'Pawball!' from the Geordie fans but the ref knew the form and took no notice and the defenders just could not cope with my speed or my ability to dodge them. I dribbled the ball past the goalkeeper and nosed it into the net, notching up one of the quickest goals in history from the centre spot. 'Goal number one!' I cried. 'Six more to go,' I thought.

Though I knew it was really beneath the dignity of dog, I decided to conform with human practice by turning two quick somersaults and then running to the touchline to grimace and gesticulate at our supporters, indicating how marvellous I was. They exploded with thousands of shouts of 'Di, Do! Di, Do! We will *never* let you go!' while the Geordie antis tried to drown them with raucous dogerwauls and dog-calls. I could take the insults but what alarmed me was when the other players on my side jumped on top of me to celebrate my goal. Suddenly I was buried under a heap of flailing human arms and legs. If I was going to get injured that was the likeliest way it would happen. Really, they should behave like grown dogs but the team manager said nothing. He just sat there on the bench, chewing gum furiously.

Clearly the Magpies didn't like it up 'em, as somebody used to say in Dog's Army, and, from then on, I was heavily marked – in more ways than one – by the Newcastle defenders. They were sadly misled by my smaller size, however, in thinking they could just brush or kick me aside. What they had to contend with, in colliding with me, was not just my sixty-five pounds of solid bone and muscle but my kinetic energy. A bullet is very small but is lethal because of its speed. Obviously footballers, whose brains are not necessarily in their heads, are not likely to be very good at physics but tangling with me at thirty miles an hour soon taught them a thing or two.

It is against my thoroughbred nature to retaliate in kind by playing dirty – the Chap's nickname for me, 'the Dirty Digger', simply refers to my condition when I have dug a hole in his garden – but I was not prepared to go on being fouled. I had established that there was nothing in the rule book about snarling so whenever one of the defenders lashed out at me with his boot I gave him a good show of teeth which usually brought him up short. When one of them complained to the ref about it I explained that I was only smiling and he couldn't prove that I wasn't. However, I felt from his manner that the ref was beginning to dislike me, probably because his efforts to keep up with me were tiring him out and he wasn't a dog-lover.

Anyway, I was soon away again but was stopped in my tracks by what I thought was the referee's whistle, blowing because I was offside or something. Even though I was standing still, a great hulking Magpie took the ball and all four paws from under me in a sliding tackle. I appealed for a foul but the ref just cried 'Play on', while the rest of the Magpies indicated that I had 'dived'. Having been deprived of the ball I asked my nearest team-mate why the ref had blown the whistle on me. 'He didn't,' he shouted, rather irascibly. 'You must be hearing things. You should have scored. You goofed.' I find it odd, in human life, how you get bawled out for doing something wrong much more loudly than you get praised for accomplishment.

Being quite good at physics myself, I quickly realised what must have happened for I had most definitely heard a high-pitched whistle. Knowing that I was going to be playing, some cunning Geordie fan must have equipped himself with one of those ultrasonic whistles and had blown it to confuse me. Being a dog, with superior hearing, I was the only one who had heard it. Well, he wouldn't catch me that way again. Nor did he. In the *Match of the Day* replay the culprit could be seen repeatedly blowing his lungs out with no sound audible, except to me and any other dogs who might be watching.

After half an hour I had scored a hat-trick which brought the stadium down. It should really have been four but one goal was, quite wrongly, disallowed by the ref. After long practice in the garden, playing with the Chap, I had learned how to pick the ball up with my mouth by getting one canine tooth firmly into the little hole where it is inflated and opening my jaws wide enough to grip the rest. Humans could probably not do it though some footballers sound as though their mouths are big enough. Anyway, I managed to get a firm grip while the ball was rather dangerously in our goal area and just romped to the other end of the field, virtually unchallenged. The crowd was silenced, in amazement, as the goalie came out at me looking full of revenge for making him look foolish three times already, but I just flicked the ball round his legs with a toss of my head and it trickled over the line as he flung himself at it, futilely, to the huge amusement of the crowd who burst into the loudest laughter I or Manchester had ever heard. I was just doing my somersaults when the ref arrived, huffing, puffing and blowing his whistle for a foul. He reached into his jersey pocket and produced a yellow card which he waved in my face.

'It's a professional foul to carry the ball like that,' he shouted.

'I'll bet you it's not in the rule book,' I countered.

'Shut up, dog, or I'll send you off for dissension,' he warned, wagging his finger at me and then awarding a goal kick.

Not long after that he blew the whistle for half-time and, as we all trooped in, the cry of 'Di, Do, Di, Do' reverberated around the stands. Even some of the Geordies were clapping me, if half-heartedly, for they knew that they had seen history made. There was no point in a pep-talk when we were leading three-nil so the manager agreed to look at the rule book to see if there was any objection to carrying the ball in the mouth. There was not but, to my annoyance, he declined to take it up with the ref. 'It would be a mistake to make him look silly,' he said. 'Human beings, and especially referees, hate losing face and he would have to withdraw your yellow card. Then he'd take it out on us one way or another. So don't provoke him by mouthing the ball again.' Sensing my disappointment, he gave me a pat and offered me a piece of chewing gum, which I declined. Dogs can see no sense in wasting energy chewing when there's nothing to swallow.

Most of the team were imbibing liquid during the break to make up for the sweat they had lost but, as we dogs have few sweat glands, I was more interested in dog-chocs, which the Chap supplied to give me energy and to keep my colour from fading. In the second half I produced two more goals, nosing one in low between the goalie's legs from a corner to take the score to five-nil, and was managing to keep possession of the ball for quite long periods, to the great annoyance of the other side, when I found that I was being substituted. I received a standing ovation as I ran off, which Cantona, who replaced me, interpreted as the welcome for him. I didn't mind too much because I had made my point and Muttson, the TV commentator, had already named me Dog of the Match.

The manager smiled as I joined him on the bench but was still too busy chewing gum and watching Cantona to say much to me except, 'We mustn't beat them by too many or there might be a riot.' After a few minutes, he took the Chap aside and whispered to him, with the Chap nodding his agreement.

'We have to leave right away,' the Chap said, seriously. 'Get your yellow collar from the dressing-room. You can keep the red one as a souvenir.'

Big deal! I thought. 'But why the rush?' I asked. I wanted to see the rest of the game.

'It's for our own safety, Dido, especially yours. The manager says that if we stay until the end of the match a gang of Geordie yobbos will be waiting for you with baseball bats for ruining their aspirations. They'll blame you for losing the Championship for them. They can already see tomorrow's headline on the sport pages – "Newcastle has gone to the dog". Even now, the manager is insisting that we have a security guard to take us to our car.'

'But these Geordies are supposed to be your people! Why should they attack us?'

'It's not just Geordies, Dido. Every team has yobbos who take their frustration out on somebody else by violence these days. Winning means so much to them that they are quite prepared to stove in the coach windows of any visiting team if they think they've had a raw deal. And you certainly gave them one today.'

Ye dogs! I thought. When I am frustrated I might be silly enough to chase my own tail a few times but I wouldn't work off my disappointment by attacking somebody else.

So, there I was, after giving a power-packed, virtuoso performance and blazing a new trail for football as well as dogdom, skulking away from the ground with my tail between my legs, like a criminal. It made no dog sense but the Chap seemed unsurprised.

'The manager's right,' he said. 'He can't afford a nasty incident that might get the club fined and barred from playing in Europe, even though it wouldn't be his fault. Football isn't just a game, these days. It's big business, with shareholders as well as managers' six-figure jobs to think about.'

Well, in that case, to hell with football! I would stick to fishing. The happy thought of a few peaceful hours on the river woke me from my reverie to see Willie hard at his clay with the facile fingers of a Dogatello. My general shape and the ball were already visible as he strove to create an antique of the future, the Chap, I fear, having already achieved that status. I snuggled down into my beanbag to watch him, but probably not for long as I felt another day-dream coming on.

You know, someone should put up a statue to whoever invented the beanbag. Perhaps Willie will be commissioned to sculpt it for the nation.

CHAPTER 2
The Making of a Superspy

I always notice strangers in our village, Kintbury in Berkshire, by their smell if not by sight, but this one was different. He was hanging round the post box and followed my Chap and me around the allotments, our usual short morning walk at about nine thirty. He used me to get into conversation with the Chap, saying that as a shooting man he had always had a Labrador, though never a chocolate one like I am. As he patted me I was slightly concerned that he might be doing a dognapping reconnaissance. There had been a lot of dognapping in our area, with some friends of mine disappearing for ever, but he did not look like a dognapper. More like a retired colonel.

I fell to wondering about him further after we returned home as I half-dozed on the lawn with a bone between my paws on that lovely September morning. Suddenly he was there claiming to have a packet of treats for me, which he must have brought with him because there is no pet shop in the village. He had knocked on the wooden back gate and the Chap had let him in. When invited to go into the house the 'Colonel', as I will call him because we never found out who or what he was, insisted on remaining in the garden out of the earshot of any eavesdroppers, human or electronic, even including the Boss, as we all call the Chap's wife.

'Sorry to appear so mysterious,' he said, 'but I have been asked to approach you on a rather delicate matter. Someone very senior in the Security Service would like to see you at the new headquarters at Millbank. Are you willing to go?'

'When do they want to see me?' the Chap asked, too eagerly I thought, for with his long involvement in the spy world, both in fact and in fiction, he was clearly sensing a story.

'Could you make three p.m. tomorrow?'

'Tomorrow! Is it that urgent?'

'It most certainly is.'

'I don't suppose that you can tell me what it is about?' the Chap asked.

'No, because I don't know and I wouldn't be allowed to tell you if I did.'

'Right! See you there then.'

'No, I won't be there,' the Colonel said, tersely. 'Someone else will be waiting for you. I don't suppose you will ever see me again. I'm a very small cog in the machine. And, by the way, be sure to take Dido with you. The person you will see is partial to dogs and is a fan of Dido, though, of course, that is off the record like everything else which has passed between us.'

I perked up immediately but the Chap looked slightly puzzled.

'It isn't just to meet Dido, is it?' he asked, knowing the lengths that some people will go to for that pleasure.

'Certainly not! Goodbye and good luck!' the Colonel replied as he waved his stick and walked out of our lives.

The Chap did not know quite what to make of it and continued to wonder all the way to London, where we were driven by the Boss next day.

A lugubrious middle-aged man, who did not reveal his name either, was waiting for us in the impressive entrance hall. M15, as most people call the Security Service, had certainly done itself proud with its new building.

'The Dame wants to see you, personally,' the man said. 'Sorry, I should have said the DG. We call her the Dame since she got her K. It's nothing to do with the pantomime that goes on here.'

The Chap smiled and was clearly chuffed, the DG being the Director General, none other than the redoubtable Dame Bella Brimmingwell herself. So that was my fan! I, too, felt chuffed.

Our man took us through the turnstile of a complete mechanical barrier which had been fitted at the back of the entrance hall so that the building could not be rushed by terrorists, like IRA bombers or Fundamentalist suicide squads. As we stood in the lift I noticed that there was no button for a thirteenth floor, but that was where we stopped because I counted the floors as we passed them. Perhaps our escort had pressed some secret gadget in his pocket.

As we were ushered into a large office smelling of new wall-to-wall carpets the Dame rose to meet us. On the wall were photographs of previous DGs and a big map of London bristling with knob-headed pins showing all the bugged foreign embassies, consulates, union headquarters, union leaders, politicians and others who automatically attracted suspicion. From his puzzled expression the Chap had clearly failed to recognise the Dame from her photographs. When these had been published after her appointment, contrary to all previous security precautions, the public had seen a woman with a short, severe haircut and here she was with a mop of hair which had been beautifully styled and permed. She also wore more make-up than her photographs had indicated and the sensible flat shoes had been replaced by stilettos, the total transformation being remarkable. Had there been a change of leadership which had not been announced? Or was the Dame in disguise and wearing a wig? No doubt, I thought, she had to be a mistress of disguise in her job, but she was not wearing any that day.

'I notice your surprise,' she said to the Chap, with a disarming smile. 'Perhaps I should explain. Many people thought I was crazy to be photographed and appear on TV telling terrorists, spies and everyone else exactly what I look like. But we are not really that stupid, you know. As soon as the pictures had been published I grew my hair long and made various other changes. I don't really need the glasses,' she said, taking them off. 'They are plain lenses.'

Suitably impressed, the Chap asked, a bit pompously I thought, 'What can I do for you?'

'It's not *your* services I require, Mr Chapman Pincher. It's Dido's.'

'Dido's!' the Chap exclaimed, unable to hide his disappointment.

'Yes. I shall need her for two or three months, if you are happy with that.'

The Chap's face fell. He looks a bit miserable at the best of times but at the thought of being deprived of me for so long his face was longer than a bass fiddle.

'You needn't worry about her. She will be with me all the time.'

'But she's not really trained as a guard dog. If that is what you need there is a wide choice at the Army dog training school at Melton Mowbray.'

I sensed that the Dame, who was clearly used to getting her way without much argument, was already becoming slightly irritated.

'I've chosen Dido because she is particularly suited to the task I have in mind, which really has nothing to do with being a guard dog. Besides, we can't bring the Army into it. We have enough trouble with our relations with them in Ulster. Anyway, I don't want any other service or department involved. You, of all people, should understand that I cannot reveal why I want her but I can tell you, in absolute secrecy, that it is for operational purposes.'

Operational! A reflex perk of my ears revealed my immediate interest. I was being called to secret service and was already wondering in what capacity. Clearly, the Dame wanted more than just a dogjective view on some knotty problem.

'I trust she will not be put in any danger,' the Chap said, anxiously.

The Dame pursed her lips. 'Hmm, no more than any dog would be in its daily life.'

'Can I be assured that she will not be taken abroad?' the Chap asked, clearly concerned that I might be trapped for six months in quarantine after my return.

'I give you my word on that. She will probably never go out of London, except at weekends when I go to my country place.'

The Chap just looked more miserable as he realised that he was in a can't-refuse situation.

'Right! We'll regard that as settled then,' the Dame said. 'From reports I have received I am sure we can trust Dido one hundred per cent,' she added, rather suggesting, I thought, that she couldn't say the same about the Chap.

'When do you want her?'

'Soonest. Her task is really urgent and there will be formalities that will take a day or two before she can begin. Couldn't you leave her now and we will send somebody down to collect her things?'

I have since regretted making my willingness to stay too obvious. The Chap was clearly hurt, especially when he realised he was not even going to be my leg-man on my missions. Of course, I would never have left the Chap on a permanent basis. It would just be sabbatical leave.

Being in the presence of a stranger the Chap restrained himself from kissing me farewell as he handed my yellow lead over and just gave me a pat. I felt really sorry for him, my own grief being totally swamped by my excitement.

When he had gone, looking more miserable than ever, I sized up the Dame more closely. In particular, I looked for the tell-tale bulge where she might have a mini-pistol in her stocking-top, but there was none. Clearly she was no Jane Bond but, then, the Chap had always told me that the officers of MI5 simply recruited the agents who did the dangerous and dirty work. I was a temporary agent recruited for a special and urgent assignment. I might even be a double agent!

The Dame pressed a button on her intercom and said, 'Dido is ready for initiation now.' Another middle-aged man appeared and took me along a corridor into a smaller room which just had the initials AA on the door.

'You will know me only as AA,' he said. 'Officers here are all known by their initials. Agents are known by cover-names and, before we go any further, we need one for you for use when we refer to you in documents.'

'"Spydo" would be too obvious, wouldn't it,' I suggested. 'How about K9007?'

'Ingenious,' he remarked. 'But the Opposition might be smart enough to work that out – after all, I could – and we don't want the Opposition to know that we have a dog on our books. The Opposition is what we always call the enemy because the Foreign Office don't like us using the word "enemy" even though they would cheerfully slit all our throats if they could.'

'Who is the Opposition?' I asked.

'I don't know. Since the Cold War ended none of us knows, except for the IRA, that is. If the IRA ever jags it in permanently, we could well be out of a job. You know your best cover could be your own name, Dido, because the Opposition would never believe that such a dog existed. I've never heard of a dog called Dido before. Fido yes, but Dido never.'

As I was to discover, charm is not MI5's line of country. Making fun of my noble name when I was called after the beautiful Queen Dido who founded the great city of Carthage and had a steamy affair with that fellow Aeneas! Anyway, who ever heard of a woman called Mata Hari before she agreed to be an agent? Now, who *hasn't* heard of her?

'However, using your own name would be against the rules so I suggest "Mars Bar",' AA said, after further thought. 'It has some relevance but not too much.'

On reflection I quite liked it because, apart from the colour connotation, I was going to be a dog of war to some extent.

'Right! Mars Bar it is for documents but only those who need to know your code-name will be told it. Inside this office, generally, you will be known by your initials – DP,' my new colleague continued.

'If the Director General is called DG why can't I be DOG?' I asked.

'You mustn't get delusions of grandeur so early,' my mentor said drily, rather suggesting, I thought, that they all did eventually.

'Then I prefer my full initials, DCP,' I said, sensing that I should make it clear from the start that, though I was amenable to discipline, I was not to be pushed around.

'OK, though it's unusual.' I felt that there was no need to tell him that I was a rather unusual dog.

'Now you'll have to go through the motions of positive vetting – just a formality in your case I'm sure, and in anybody's really because it has never prevented a spy getting in here, but we do have to go through the motions in case there is ever a cock-up leading to questions in Parliament.'

Positive vetting! I must say that I did not like the sound of that for the thought of a vet always gives me the shivers. However, I did my best not to show it.

'Right, DCP,' AA said, producing a form, 'I have to ask you a few questions.'

They were simple enough and hardly worth bothering with because, after the publication of my first two volumes, my life is literally an open book. I had to be a British-born subject of British parents, which I was. In fact, with my distant Canadian ancestry, near Labrador, my credentials were immaculate. Having produced seven puppies it was obvious that I was not a homosexual, though that does not seem to be quite so important these days. I was not likely to have a drink or drug problem. I was not involved with any suspect political party and was immune to the main human inducement to treachery – money. In fact there is nothing treacherous whatever in the nature of dog.

I signed the Official Secrets Act with my pawprint and that was it.

'Am I now an accredited agent?' I asked.

'You are.'

'Shouldn't a female agent be called an "alady"?' I asked.

'I don't get it,' AA replied.

I was not surprised because I had already decided that he was not that bright.

'There is something I should have told you before you signed up,' AA said. 'If anything goes wrong you are on your own and we will disown you and deny everything. Everything we do has to be deniable, especially in Parliament.'

Now he tells me! I thought, but said nothing.

'Will I be licensed to kill?' I asked. 'At least to defend myself?'

'You have to be joking. None of us are. Ever since that Dick Black took over in the f it's been like the Civil Service here, only worse. Don't you know we a pposed to be accountable? A secret service accountable to a Parliament that has always been riddled with subversives, if not spies, is crazy in my book! We can't even do a burglary without a warrant signed by the Home Secretary and you know how soft they always are.'

I was beginning to wish I hadn't come.

'But am I in any danger of being killed?'

'I suppose we all are, certainly by the IRA, who are no respecters of dogs or people, but it's part of the job, part of being patriotic.'

I felt a surge of pride. Breathes there the dog with soul so dead . . . Greater love hath no dog than that she lays down her life for her country . . . Ask not what dogdom can do for you but what you can do for dogdom . . . I would put my life in their paws.

'Right, I will now hand you over to another department for instruction in trade-craft,' AA said.

'What's that?'

'Our methods of undercover work. They are very secret, which is why I got you to sign that document first.' Then, becoming really matey for the first time, he said, 'I'll give you a few bits of advice from my personal experience. Always treat anything that anybody tells you with reserve. It may not be true.'

'What, even in here?' I asked.

'Especially in here! You should know, too, that there are people here who will resent you. We are all trained to be intensely suspicious of all strangers. That's the way we are made. You'll go that way yourself if you stay here any length of time. You will also find that most people hate each other here. I suppose it's because we've all made such awful boobs that we have no respect for each other. In your case many of them will also be jealous that you are working with the DG. There's one fat slob, in particular, to be wary of – AC. Frankly, I don't know how he survives. He's always laying eggs – that's our secret term for making mistakes. AC has achieved the impossible by laying the same egg twice on several occasions. I suspect that they're afraid that if they fired him he would move to Australia and write his memoirs. Anyway, steer clear of him! He's bad news. He could foul up your operation.'

My next colleague was not AC but AB and was almost indistinguishable from the first except that he smoked a pipe which fell from his mouth when told by AA that I belonged to the Chap.

'Not Pincher!' he said, aghast.

'I'm afraid so,' AA replied. 'It's the Dame's idea. Apparently we are in a shit or bust situation.'

'To have involved Pincher we have to be,' AB commented, lugubriously. AA had a point, though. M15 must have wanted me desperately to bring themselves to involve the Chap after his connection with that *Spycatcher* fellow.

Clearly, AB was going to tell me the minimum and every time he told me anything he muttered to himself, 'Does she really need to know?' He ended up telling me a few things but nothing that had not already been done to death in spy novels. He warned me always to sit in the centre of a room and never near a column or a pillar because it might be bugged, and always to be suspicious of a pepper-pot or a vase of flowers for the same reason. He showed me how to see through a frosted window by putting sellotape on it and how to listen at keyholes by putting my ear to them. He started to tell me how to avoid being tailed by doubling back on the Underground, running up the down escalator and jumping on and off buses and into taxis before he realised that I would never have any money on me. He said that to resist interrogation if I was captured I should stay zip-lipped and say nothing, least of all my code-name, initials, rank and number. I had no rank and no number. He then warned me about the danger of being recruited by the Opposition as a double agent.

'The word you must always remember is MICE!'

'Mice?' I repeated, in some amazement.

'No, MICE,' he replied, his trained ear sensing the difference. 'M, I, C and E are the initials for the temptations that may be put your way. They stand for Money, Ideology, which is usually political, Compromise, usually meaning sexual blackmail, and Ego, implying the kick which some people get out of spying, though God knows why. If ever you are tempted don't lie back and think about England, sit up and think about MICE.'

He ended his briefing by explaining the difference between intelligence spelled with a small 'i' and with a big 'I'.

'In this place you will find that they are not necessarily connected,' he added, drily. Melting slightly, he then said, 'I'll give you a tip from my own experience – common events have common causes so don't waste your time looking for esoteric explanations. The simplest explanation is usually the right one. For instance, if a Top Secret file goes missing don't assume that a spy has stolen it. The odds are that it is in one of the loos where some officer has been reading it.'

I was then taken to the Technical Department, which was closely linked with the Department of Dirty Tricks, and left in the hands of AD to whom I was introduced as 'our latest asset', which I regarded as a compliment, though it might have been tongue-in-cheek. The initials were already becoming rather confusing but AD looked different from the others. In fact I thought he looked rather sloshed.

'Is this where you keep the cloaks and daggers?' I asked, partly in jest.

'Neither exists,' AD replied, wearily. 'You will probably find intelligence work unbearably dull most of the time. As for the James Bond blondes, most of my dates have been with a desk,' he said with a sigh. 'Right now we have to fit you out with your identity chip. The ear, I think, will be the best place.'

'Where's yours?' I asked, with some concern.

'Oh! we just have a card which lets us through the electronic barrier in the hall and then lets us into our own office but nobody else's. You won't ever forget yours,' rather suggesting that he sometimes did.

Without too much pain he slid a minuscule microchip under the skin inside my left ear. The things I do for England!, as Henry the Eighth is supposed to have said when he got into bed with Anne of Cleves.

'There!' AD exclaimed as he wiped my ear with his handkerchief, which looked none too clean. 'We must never underrate the Opposition. They are perfectly capable of dyeing a dog chocolate and trying to infiltrate her in here with bugs planted all over her. You will be "swept" from time to time to make sure that the Opposition has not managed to bug you.'

I nodded my acceptance of this imposition.

'From time to time you may also have to swallow this,' he said, showing me something that was clearly disguised as a fat, cooked sausage made out of brown plastic. 'The front is a microphone and the rear is a tape-recorder. Nobody ever expects a dog to be fitted with a tape-recorder. Make sure you swallow it rear end first and, whatever you do, don't bite it. It's not expendable. You will be expected to return it when you leave.'

Both ends looked the same, as they do with any sausage, but I could see no point in raising that. I sniffed it and it smelled of nothing.

'It's very high tech, state of the art in fact,' AD explained, stroking the sausage with some admiration.

'In what way?'

'It automatically eliminates stomach rumbles and other background noises.'

I looked suitably impressed.

'We used to call it a "hot dog",' he said, continuing to stroke it with unrestrained affection, 'but, this morning, we all received a directive forbidding us to use that name. I see why now. They don't want to give you the opportunity of sueing the Service for compensation for "hurt feelings".'

I was about to say 'What rubbish!' but realised that, as the Chap has always advised, I should keep all my options open. So I simply nodded my head without committing myself.

AD then produced an extensible dog lead and collar to go with it.

'I've got one of those,' I said. 'It enables me to do long-distance sniffs when I'm out with the Chap.'

'This is rather different,' AD assured me, condescendingly. 'There's a microphone in the collar and a conducting wire in the lead. Someone can take you into a pub and let you wander round the tables where things are being discussed that we might like to overhear. Spies often set up meetings in pubs or use them for drops.'

'Drops of what?' I asked. 'Whisky?'

'Drops, my dear girl, are places where spies leave secret messages.'

He then showed me a mini-camera so small that it, too, could be inserted into the collar and he set it aside with the rest of my equipment which would be handed over to the Dame.

'I'll give you a useful tip I learned for myself,' he said, as he finished his briefing. 'Always pick up book matches. They help you to recall where you were last night. Sometimes you will find that you have made a note on them, such as a telephone number. Then you can ring it and find out what it was.'

I saw the virtue of this wisdom, especially for someone in his condition.

As he conducted me to the Dame's office, carrying my kit of equipment, he revealed that there was another secret department which I might have to visit one day – 'Cover Plans', where a team of experts worked full-time on ingenious methods of concealing cock-ups. As we stood, silently, in the lift I wondered about my role. Was I to be involved in rooting out another traitor in the midst of MI5? The Sixth Man, perhaps? Or might it be the First Woman?

The Dame welcomed me with a friendly pat and settled me down for my ultra-confidential briefing.

'Right, Dido – I am going to call you that rather than use stupid initials, which is a practice set up long before I came here. My problem is one which I could not possibly reveal to any other person, not even to my Deputy, which is why I chose a dog. Having read your books I decided that it just had to be you in spite of your unfortunate association with someone who has been anathema here ever since the *Spycatcher* affair. Until now I haven't confided in anyone and I am sure that you will understand why when I explain my appalling situation to you.'

I preened myself, though I hope not noticeably, and looked at the Dame with intense attention.

'Soon after I took over here everything began to leak – our current operations, our forward plans, the names of our agents, even the secret menus in the canteen. We began to get play-backs from a foreign power indicating that they knew everything we were doing . . .'

'What was the foreign power?' I interrupted.

'You mustn't ask me questions like that,' she said, sharply. 'I can only tell you what you need to know.'

I gestured my apology and the Dame continued.

'At first I thought it must be some disaffected officer who resented being subservient to a woman and wanted me to fail – there's a lot of that about. So I made a big chart of all the leaks and compared them with lists of those who knew the particular secrets.' She stared at me in silence for a moment, then blurted out, 'I have reluctantly concluded that there is only one person who can be doing all the leaking.'

'Who's that?' I asked, chancing my leg.

'Me,' she replied.

'You?' I reiterated in astonishment.

'Yes, me and me alone. Because of our strict need-to-know policy I was the only one who knew all the secrets. Obviously I am the only one who has to know everything.'

I waited for her to tell me more. It was beginning to look like she might be the First Woman. She leaned towards me as though it were painful to continue.

'I'm sure I don't have to tell you that I am not a spy and in fact I have not told anybody anything, not even the Prime Minister whom I see from time to time. When I am not in the office I am alone most of the time so there is nobody to leak to even if I wanted to.'

I remembered the advice about treating everything I was told with reserve, and about MICE. I couldn't see the Dame being a double agent for Money. She must have plenty of take-home pay for such a prestigious job with such responsibility and just did not look like a woman who would be greedy for more. As for Ideology, she seemed a thoroughly good democratic Brit devoted to the generally accepted principle that all are equal but some are more equal than others. Compromise? She did not look as though she would be fooled by the charms of any professional Romeo. As for Ego, hers already had maximum expression through being in charge of so many male spooks. I dismissed any doubts about her loyalty as she continued.

'I wondered if I might be talking in my sleep – I always sleep alone, of course – and the bedroom might be bugged in spite of all our precautions. I had it swept and re-swept but the leaks have continued.'

I was rapt in attention. For a moment my thoughts strayed to the Chap. What he would have given to be a spy on the wall!

The Dame dabbed her eyes with a handkerchief, being careful with her mascara which, as part of her deception plan, was rather thick.

'As an experiment I even made some things up, invented some phoney agents and told nobody about them, but they still leaked! It's as though the Opposition is somehow reading my thoughts. Of course, some of my senior colleagues see the play-backs from intelligence reports and statements by defectors. So, naturally, they are beginning to suspect that I am a spy and not a very clever one at that, though none has had the guts yet to say so.'

I felt a great surge of sympathy. Clearly we were up against something really big and inscrutable. Just two females together, confronting perhaps the greatest counter-espionage challenge ever faced by MI5!

She dabbed her eyes again and I saw that, in spite of her precautions, the mascara was beginning to run.

'I'm sure I'm being followed by our own watchers. Too many people are staring at shop windows or speaking into walkie-talkies whenever I turn round suddenly. And whenever I pick up my phone my experienced ears can hear deep breathing. Could there be anything more ignominious? So, you can see how I need your assistance.'

'How can I help?' I asked, feeling very sorry for this fellow female in such distress.

'Well, the first thing we have to do is for you to establish, as a completely objective observer, whether I am talking in my sleep. The opposition may have invented some listening device which is undetectable by our sweepers. They've done that before.'

'But couldn't the Technical Department just fit you up with a tape-recorder?' I asked.

The Dame gave me a look close to contempt.

'What excuse could I give? They know nothing about my private life and they'd think I was up to some sexual deviation, you know, like mirrors in the ceiling. Some kind soul would be round to the newspapers in no time. I just couldn't risk it. Anyway, I don't trust the Technical Department. It's headed by the man who thought he was going to get my job and 'fit me up' is exactly what he might do. And there is another reason why I couldn't involve another department.'

'What is that?' I asked, feeling that it was safe to do so.

'Always remember Richard Nixon,' she answered, raising a forefinger and wagging it. 'He was ruined by tapes. If nobody else had been involved he could have destroyed them.'

She certainly had a point there.

'So what do we do?'

'When we get home you'll have to swallow this,' she said, withdrawing the erstwhile 'hot dog' from my equipment pack. 'In fact you'll have to do it every day.' She, too, stroked it with affection indicating its popularity throughout the Establishment where, presumably, it must have rendered signal service on many assignments. 'I will, of course, wash and sterilise it each time,' she added. I refrained from pointing out that we dogs are not as fussed about our own body fluids as humans are, to an extent which puzzles us.

'You will sleep in my room – your beanbag has already arrived – and each morning, when we have recovered the sausage, I will wash it, play it back and then erase it,' the Dame continued.

To cut a pong story short, the experiment was negative. The Dame never said a word in her sleep. There were a few moans and she snored a bit, though no more than most of us. Briefly, I wondered if she could be, unwittingly, snoring in code but remembered the advice against looking for overcomplicated solutions. We kept going for three nights and the tapes must have been the most boring ever recorded.

Obviously dismayed, the Dame said, 'Nevertheless, we must persevere. It's our only hope. If I don't solve the problem soon I will have to resign. It's just lucky that there hasn't been a war with the Opposition recently.'

I felt deeply sorry for her and was determined to do everything I could to solve her, and the nation's, problem. Two heads are better than one, even if one of them is only human, I thought, but did not say it.

From then on I went everywhere with her, complete with the 'hot dog' unobtrusively inside me, both inside and outside the MI5 building – on shopping trips, to the doctor's, to church (with a special dispensation from the vicar), even to the hairdresser's. Always the ostensible reason for my presence was the same: because of the perpetual danger of terrorist attack she needed a guard dog and, for deception purposes, it shouldn't look like one.

We were getting nowhere fast and the leaks were avalanching when my windfall came. I had learned that MI5 relied heavily on windfalls – chance occurrences – and it was at the hairdresser's that mine came though, of course, the mind has to be astute enough to appreciate any significance in chance events which a lesser intellect might just dismiss, if they registered them at all. The hairdresser who had styled the Dame's hair and kept it in band-box condition through regular visits was called Alphonse. He looked gay and probably was, which is common enough in that trade, and was no relation, I learned, to the well-known Lucky Alphonse who specialised in middle partings. Each time we went for a set or a blow-dry I noticed that as soon as the Dame got her head under the enormous hairdryer she nodded off to sleep, even though Alphonse always brought her a cup of tea. When I ribbed her about it she said that she never slept so soundly as she did under the drier and it was that chance remark which gave me my clue.

Until then I had been in the habit of curling up and having a nap myself for it was enough, or so we had thought, that the sausage inside me was fully alert. So I decided that on the next visit I would just pretend to be asleep and keep my eyes open. As soon as the Dame was nodding away after her cup of tea I saw Alphonse signal to a confederate who wheeled in a trolley from another room bearing several electronic 'black boxes' connected by a thick cable which he plugged into a socket on the dome of the hairdryer. There was a whirring sound which had not been picked up by the sausage because it had been eliminated as background noise – a case of a gadget being too clever by half. Then, shortly before Alphonse gently awakened the Dame with the news that her hair was dry, the cable was disconnected and the trolley was wheeled away from the salon.

Immediately I felt I had the solution in the palm of my paw. It had all been too surreptitious to have anything to do with drying hair. I said nothing until we were back in the office, when I asked, 'Do you ever feel funny after that cup of tea they give you at the hairdresser's?'

She thought a moment, then said, 'I get a bit of a headache but I put it down to the heat of the dryer.'

'Not so,' I said. 'You've been drugged.'

She was disinclined to believe it until I told her about the apparatus and my suspicion that the whole thing was a state-of-the-art brain-scanner for reading her thoughts. While they had been washing the outside of her head with shampoo they had given the inside a thorough brain-wash electronically. The more we thought about it the more it fitted the facts.

'Right,' she said. 'Just leave it to me now and not a word to anyone.'

The rest of my information is largely conjecture because I was thenceforth studiously excluded from the inquiries on the basis of need-to-know, but what I gathered was this:

MI5 officers carried out a night raid on the hairdresser's during a weekend and removed the whole apparatus for examination, taking other equipment and goods to make it look like an ordinary burglary. They confirmed my suspicion that it was a highly effective thought-reading machine which was entirely new to British science as well as to the espionage world. Though the Dame never admitted it and would tell me nothing I could sense by her whole change of mood that her problem was solved. There was also the tell-tale fact that I was never asked to swallow the sausage again, which was just as well as it was showing signs of wear and was in need of maintenance.

I racked my brains wondering what nationality Alphonse might be but that led nowhere. He could have been anything and probably was. He might have been recruited by a quite different power for M for money. So I never did discover what the foreign power which had invented the brain-scanner was because there was never a court case. Nobody was arrested and, unless it was done surreptitiously, nobody was deported. I strongly suspect that once MI5 had unravelled the intricacies of the machine they decided to keep the entire episode secret because they wanted to use the apparatus themselves on unsuspecting people. Anyway, my story un-doubtedly explains why the Dame immediately reverted to short back and sides because she could never trust a hair dryer again or any hairdresser.

As for MI5's gratitude to me, well let the facts speak for themselves. They could not get rid of me quickly enough, and I mean rid of.

'There's someone waiting in the hall to take you home,' the Dame said, unexpectedly. 'I've enjoyed our acquaintance. All the best to you!'

I wondered if it might be the Chap or perhaps the Colonel but when I got there it was a very fat man with a red face and thick lips who introduced himself as AC, the man against whom I had been warned. I distrusted him from the start but had no option but to get into his car. As the afternoon was very sunny and hot I asked for the windows to be opened.

It was not long before I realised that we were driving north out of London. 'You are going the wrong way,' I said. 'I live down the M4.' Naturally, I became concerned when all he did was to turn his perspiring face to me with an evil leer as he drove on.

After a few more miles he stopped at a lay-by to remove his jacket when I saw, to my dismay, that he was wearing a shoulder holster with a nasty-looking handgun. So that was why they kept AC on in spite of his boobs! He was the one man licensed to kill and the one man prepared to do it. He was MI5's bumper-offer and was taking me for a ride because I knew too much and might tell the Chap about something they regarded as of supreme importance to national security. I was out of the window in a flash and up the embankment. AC was quick on the draw and fired one shot but the slug (meaning either AC or the bullet) missed. He had laid yet another egg and would be in serious trouble when he returned to head-quarters, though I felt sure that the Dame knew nothing whatever about this crude attempt to silence me. AC leaned out and was about to fire another shot but he was too late. The noise of the first report had woken me up with a start and he and everyone else in my bone-dream had vanished.

What a relief! It was so good to be back on the lawn at home in the real world with a real bone instead of a fake sausage and the *demi-monde* of MI5, which is far too devious a place for a simple country girl like me.

CHAPTER 3
Reluctant Premier

I can truthfully claim that I have worked long and hard for the rights of dog, as my previous books record, and the possibility of representing my species in the British Parliament had possessed me to such an extent that the Chap had made inquiries about the legal situation regarding the adoption of a dog as a Parliamentary candidate. My feeling was that if people like Screaming Lord Sutch could stand then why couldn't I, especially as I could afford the deposit out of the royalties on my books, which are still paid into my own bank account. We failed to get a straight answer out of the Westminster officials, who just brushed us off, and I suppose that it was the inequity of that response, along with all the research I had done in case I might qualify, which sparked off my fantastic adventure.

I had stood in a by-election for the Isle of Dogs and had won with a landslide. A pedigree dog who is also an Establishment figure has to be a Tory and I was elected in a predominantly Labour constituency because the voters were in the mood to show their scorn for all the parties. My personal dogifesto had been simple and easy to understand – everything for everybody at no cost to them – and they had loved it. I had promised to chew through all red tape and had licked a lot of babies which, unlike most politicians, I really love, and, as there were a lot of immigrants in the area, I suppose that my chocolate colour also helped.

One does not have to be in the House of Commons long to realise one's impotence and that the reputation of the Mother of Parliaments for the importance of its debates in the 'democratic process' is just a myth. No backbencher's speech, however brilliant or constructive, has any effect if the Government has a large majority and knows how to use it. So why should an ordinary MP, canine or human, bother to speak except, perhaps, to let off some pent-up steam? Deluded by my heady election experience – the media had hailed me as 'a brilliant barker who could hold crowds smellbound' – I fitted the Chap's definition of politicians: those who believe they have done something when they have only said something, Parliament being something of a fantasy world largely inhabited by people who cannot run their own lives but believe they can govern everybody else's. However, soon after I had actually taken my beanbag in the Commons I returned to reality and settled down to sleep, like the rest of the backbenchers, waking up to join the occasional 'yah yahs' and the boos or to waddle into the voting lobby as required and never putting a paw wrong because I had never said anything, except once to complain of a draught. Furthermore, while I had never experienced one, the whip held extra significance for me.

As nothing that I had promised the voters was likely to be accomplished before the next election I would expect to lose my beanbag but I was so disenchanted that, frankly, it would be a happy release. So I suppose I would have remained in a coma, enjoying the Club privileges like the subsidised food and drink, had not Fate, in the form of a few Eurosceptic backbenchers and some embittered Lords – what I called the Gang of Ten – had other ideas. In November, when the leadership always becomes open to challenge according to the self-destructive Tory rules, they decided to use me as a stalking dog to challenge John Minor for the Premiership. Stupidly, though I suppose I was flattered, being excessively vain, like all MPs, I had allowed my name to go forward to get them off my back and nobody was more amazed than they were, apart from myself, when I won the first ballot with another landslide.

I usually aim for the top in anything I do but the Premiership was a job I did not want. Who in dog's name would fancy it with the media gunning remorselessly for anyone in authority anywhere and banana skins lurking everywhere, often being surreptitiously positioned by one's own colleagues?

However, as the Gang of Ten had only put me there as a stop-yap, because they thought they could get rid of me easily when it suited them, I was determined to make a go of it. I was my country's first canine Prime Minister, like Elizabeth the First was the first virgin Queen, and I vowed that when they got shot of John Minor just for spite and the sake of change they would see some likeness and regret ignoring the ancient wisdom that a dog you know is always better than a bitch you don't know.

When I arrived at Buckingham Palace to kiss paws I received a rather mixed reception from the royal corgis who were very put out when the Queen told me that Labradors were really her favourite breed, which I already knew from several sources. She even went so far as to say that she trusted her canine Labs more than any human Labs, Libs or Lib-Labs. I had been presented to Her Majesty when she had visited our village in 1995. She had read my books and had written to congratulate me about one of them so we had a lot in common and I greatly looked forward to our regular Tuesday evening twosomes when we could bone each other up on various matters of State and girlie talk. That would be one worthwhile recompense for taking on the awesome job which presented me with immediate problems.

First, I had to select a Cabinet and I hadn't a clue how to do it. None of the MPs I had listened to in my waking moments had impressed me. Obviously, I couldn't consult any of my Parliamentary colleagues because they would just have suggested themselves or their pals. I had heard the Chap say that any Prime Minister must be a good butcher so I consulted the only butcher I know, Colin who runs our village butcher's shop which has the nostalgic name of 'Thatchers'.

The only one of the old Cabinet I was determined to save was Mrs German Shephard because she belongs to a breed that is useful in a tight corner, even if not entirely reliable. 'Give five of these the chop, Colin,' I said, as I pawed him the full list of the last Cabinet, excluding Mrs Shephard. Cleaver in hand, he read out the names of John Bummer, Virginia Topless, Patrick Maystew, Michael Blossomtime, Michael Portfolio . . .

'That's sufficient,' I said. 'It'll be difficult enough finding replacements for that lot.'

I was determined that none of the Gang of Ten who had set me up would get any preferment. Using my power of patronage, I would give the backbenchers knighthoods but only because that was a public brand showing that they would never get anywhere politically. For my Cabinet I picked out five other backbenchers with names which reminded me of dogs or who happened to look like them, making sure that there were a couple of women who looked like bitches among them. Why I should have included the women, apart from the need to assuage the feminists, I cannot think. If anyone was going to resent a female being in command it would be them. I would have liked to include Enoch Poodle, who has visited my house, simply because he is nobody's poodle and never has been, always being his own dog, but he was not eligible, having lost his beanbag.

The next problem was much more difficult: an agenda for my first Cabinet meeting. As there had been no general election there was no party dogifesto so I had to generate some idea that would really grab the voters' interest and get me off to a good start with the media. But what? I had not had time to appoint the Seven Wise Dogs who, I had always intended, would replace the Seven so-called Wise Men who had long advised the Government, with results which all could see. So I decided to consult Saint Bernard Ingham, Lady Thatcher's former chef-de-kitchen-cabinet who had the nearest name to a breed I could trust and looked like one, too, in his rugged way, though some say he looks more like a bulldog. 'Why don't you pop round and see Maggie?' he responded, briskly. (Little did I know that she had foreseen my call to him and had put him up to making the suggestion.)

Naturally, I was round smartly to see the Great Lady for advice, in absolute secrecy and confidentiality of course, as one bitch to another. That meant dodging the reporters who were always hanging around in Downing Street hoping for crises or the means of inventing them, which I did by using the garden door leading on to the recently renamed Dog Guards Parade.

'We are so glad you've come,' Maggie said, extending a hand graciously. 'We were hoping you would. We were so pleased with your Cabinet changes. Quite inspired! You must have spent a lot of time over them.'

I did not enlighten her, but said, 'Could you help me by suggesting an agenda for my first Cabinet meeting? I have to confess I am rather stuck for ideas.'

'That's always a problem, my dear, for any Cabinet meeting. You have to think of something that will occupy the time and make your colleagues think they are being consulted when they are not, while not giving them any cause for stalking out in a huff and resigning.'

I nodded my acceptance of that valuable advice, based, like everything else she dispensed, on bitter experience.

'You see the whole business is based on a nonsense,' she went on. 'The very basis of democracy – one person, one vote – is founded on the delusion that all people, and all dogs of course, are created equal. In reality every person, like every dog, is different and entitled to believe that she or he is better than the next, and some obviously are. Just look at *us*! If politicians did not believe that why would any of them compete in elections where they always claim that they are miles better than the others?'

I had not come for a lecture and felt that she might be practising on me for some forthcoming lucrative tour of the American women's clubs, so I interposed, 'On the immediate subject for my agenda . . .'

'Well, it's rather short notice but I am sure we can give you some general guidance,' she replied, rather grandly I thought. 'You need something of universal interest that will make you popular with the voters and, of course, with the cartoonists – that's very important. It really helps to be cartoonable. I think you probably are,' she added, eyeing me up and down, loftily. 'At the same time, so that you can concentrate on home affairs which are what really matter vote-wise, you must find a way of sidelining the Europeans who will, otherwise, occupy all your time and take you out of London.' Her mood hardened as she added, bitterly, 'That's when the traitors strike, you know. When you are out of the country.'

I nodded my understanding, but had no intention of ever leaving Britain because of the quarantine restrictions, though I imagine they could be fiddled, like anything else, for the country's leader.

'So try to think of something that will occupy the Europeans, my dear, and irritate them, if possible,' Lady Thatcher continued, smiling broadly. 'Yes, *irritate* them. We do so enjoy irritating the Europeans, especially the Frogs, don't you? And particularly that awful Jacques Deloo, as we always called him in private, though he is not around now. The Frogs have never forgiven us since Agincourt and hate us even more for rescuing them in the last war. They will never forgive us for *that*, you may be sure. So just annoy them all so much that they lose their cool and can't think straight. That's how we got our way with them.'

'But how would I do that?' I asked, perhaps a little plaintively.

'Just keep shaking your head. You can do that can't you? Everyone, even the Greeks, understands that gesture. Then always vote No! No! No! I promise you they literally won't be able to make head or tail of you. Nothing personal in that remark, of course.'

I could see that no specific idea for an agenda was forthcoming so I prepared to leave.

'Thank you very much, Lady Thatcher,' I said reverentially.

'Please call us Margaret – I don't really like Maggie, though it was useful on the hustings I suppose, making us sound down to earth – and do come again. Would you like a drink before you go? We always have one about this time.'

She pressed a bell and Denis came in to join us, in plus-fours and carrying a huge golf-bag. He seemed very nice. A pity I didn't have a canine Denis to lean on.

'Don't forget,' she said sharply, as I departed, 'don't give anyone grounds for calling you any European's poodle, least of all that awful Santer who looks like being worse than Deloo.'

It was not a well chosen remark, particularly to a chocolate Labrador of my standing.

Back in Number Ten I racked my brains and got nowhere until, lying in the bath, which was the only think-tank available to me because of all the public spending cuts made by John Minor, the idea flashed into my mind. Good old Maggie! It was her mention of Jacques Deloo that must have sparked it off. I knew right away that my idea fulfilled all her requirements brilliantly. It would raise a novel issue which impacted on everyone's lives in the most personal manner. The cartoonists of every nation would love it and it would cause controversy throughout Europe, keeping the bureaucrats busy and out of real mischief for years.

My plan was to demand the harmonisation – yes, that was the word – of all the public loos in the European Community! From the exact size and shape of the seats – big enough to accommodate the likes of Chancellor Kohl but small enough to prevent any child falling through – the height of the pedestals, the precise curve of the S-bends, the length of the chains (if fitted) and the number of links in them, the decibel noise of the cisterns – all would have to be identical in every town and village throughout the Community under pain of being heavily fined or having offending loos closed down, which would create severe political as well as physical discomfort. How the bureaucrats would love it! The work it would create! I would be the toast of Brussels and could become the patron saint of plumbers throughout Europe.

Britain would lead the campaign for the EWC and the Frogs would hate it. Just imagine! The traditional French pissoir, which is such a Gallic emblem, could no longer be round but would have to be rectangular. Nor could it be green but would have to be bright yellow, like all the rest. A green loo might blend into the background but that is exactly what a loo should not do when needed at short notice. It would also be forbidden for heads to show above the parapet and – this would be the killer – as both essential services had to be offered in the same building the purely stand-up convenience, such as the pissoir, would be banned. This would be essential to avoid sex discrimination, for why should a female, who might be *in extremis* and spot a convenience in the nick of time, be barred from making use of it? No, under my scheme all Euroloos would have to be open to females who should be entitled to stand up if they wished while both sexes should have the choice of sitting down at all times. There would be the same standard charge for both sexes everywhere, eventually payable in uro-money. The squatting loo, where nothing is provided but a hole in the floor, and which still persists in many parts of Europe, would be outlawed completely. No doubt in more remote areas squatters' rights movements would arise, probably with their usual quota of violence, but that pitfall would have to be faced.

The first move, before any physical changes were made, would be to give all public lavatories the same name throughout Europe so that anyone travelling in any country could see exactly where each was, quickly, in an emergency. I had always thought that 'toilet' and its foreign counterparts were horrible words. And I knew exactly what the new name should be, a perfect technical description and one that would really bug the Frogs, as Maggie had suggested – Waterloo! Everyone everywhere knows what water and loo mean and imagine that word, Napoleon's ultimate defeat, being given permanent publicity in every town and village in Europe! The French would fight so hard to stop it that it would occupy the European agenda for years, with various countries siding with France and others with me. To call it anything else on any signpost or notice would be another fineable offence.

As I relaxed there in the bath I felt deeply gratified on behalf of my species. It had needed a dog free from all inhibitions about natural functions to make this long-needed stand – or sit, whichever might be preferred – for the rights of man, woman and child. I shook myself dry and felt really elated as I bounded down the Number Ten main staircase, where the side-wall would one day be graced by my photograph, and knew I had to tell Maggie about it without delay.

'A stunning project!' she remarked. 'I wish we'd thought of it. It really does get to the bottom of things. You'll start a chain reaction throughout the Community. The Frogs will refer it to the European Court of Human Rights and that will take ages. Well done, Dido, if I may call you that!'

I smiled my assent, trying to imitate her graciousness.

'There will, of course, be the usual rackets,' she warned, raising her finger. 'The so-called poorer members of the Community will expect grants to build the new Waterloos and they'll claim for hundreds that don't exist, like the Italians do for olive groves. And they'll try to get money by sit aside, squat aside and suchlike.'

'I had thought of that,' I said. 'We'll have to have inspectors, and that will be good for jobs.'

'Who are you going to put in charge of the project here?' she asked. 'You'll have to delegate it you know. Don't try to do everything yourself like I did.'

'I think that it is an obvious job for the Privy Council', I said. 'They don't seem to have much to do.'

'Capital! It will give the name some meaning at last, after all these years. You might even get the Privy Purse to pay for it. You may find that it was set up for that kind of purpose in the first place, in which case it will be back to basics. Or should I say fundamentals?'

Flushed with success, I had visions of Dido being immortalised through the name Waterloo, alongside Napoleon and Wellington.

'Just one thing,' Maggie warned, raising her finger again. 'Watch out for leaks – sorry about the pun. You can't trust anyone these days, civil servants in particular. They leak all over the place.'

I was trying to visualise that revolting scene of mass incontinence in Whitehall when Maggie brought the meeting to an end by saying, 'We don't want to see all your good work consigned to the pan – I mean the dustbin – of history, do we? So watch out for leaks!'

That afternoon, as I left Number Ten for the House to face my first Prime Minister's Question Time, I felt confident about the future. I could easily bark the Opposition down at the Despatch Box, even at the risk of being called 'strident', but, out in the street, I found the media in force behind the barrier: reporters and photographers from the newspapers, TV and radio, with those obscene, hairy microphones. They shouted, repeatedly, 'When are you going to resign?' 'Are you going to the Palace to hand in your resignation now?' Declining to be accosted in the street like some tart, as other Prime Ministers had foolishly allowed themselves to be, I did not respond, jumped into my car and just looked straight ahead as my bodyguard slammed the door. But what were they all on about? Resign? I had hardly started.

The packed House was hushed as I entered. At a sign from Madam Speaker, the grim-looking Labour leader asked what seemed a pointless question: 'When is the Prime Minister going to visit Crapstone and Piddlehinton?' My civil service advisers had warned me that it must be the apparently innocuous precursor of some more dangerous supplementary question but, being not of this world, had failed to find any allusion in the names of two obscure villages, one on the edge of Dartmoor, the other in Dorset. I suppose I should have smelled something, especially with my nose, but I'm not a devious dog by nature.

'I have no plans to visit Crapstone or Piddlehinton,' I replied.

Then, with a gleeful look, as though poised for a kill, Her Majesty's Leader of the Opposition delivered the artful supplementary: 'Could the Right Honourable Bitch tell us why she is ruining our relations with Europe for the sake of a uro-gimmick? Is she aware that, at this moment, the French President is besieged in the Elysée Palace by a raging mob chanting "Pas de pissoirs: pas de pouvoir!" Another mob is blockading the French exit from the Channel tunnel. All trains to the tunnel out of Waterloo' – he leered at me as he said the name – 'have been cancelled because it is unsafe for any Briton to travel to the Continent. Furthermore. . .'

Someone tried to pass me a copy of the *Evening Standard* bearing the headline, in huge type, DIDO'S WATERLOO, followed by the inevitable *double entendre* 'Premier's Secret Leaks', but I was too flabbergasted to read it and just sat slumped on my beanbag. The Labour leader banged on with various other aquatic allusions dragging in every relevant, clapped-out cliché, with only 'the wind of change' missing. It was all too obvious that my precious project had somehow leaked to the Opposition and they had leaked it to the French and to the media. I looked up at the Press gallery and saw that those who had cheered me in their headlines when I had won the leadership contest now couldn't wait to knock me down.

My brain worked fast. Why had Maggie warned me about the danger of leaks? Had she leaked it? Had she not wanted another female Prime Minister to succeed? It was an unkind thought and I dismissed it as out of character, though in the political world anything now seemed possible. Surely it couldn't have been Denis, though golfers do gossip on the greens?

'The violent, anti-British reaction to this crude anti-European ploy has backfired,' the Labour leader ranted. Then, adopting a Churchillian pose, he shouted, 'The storm will not be confined to France. From Stockholm in the north to Athens in the south, from Lisbon in the west to Berlin in the east, in public lavatories all over Europe there are rumblings of imminent thunder . . .'

'There always are,' I tried to say, aware that there's nothing like a belly-laugh for defusing a Parliamentary row, but I was inaudible. My adversary was thumping the table crying, 'And it's all the British Prime Minister's fault! She is responsible for the whole outrageous catastrophe, or should I say dogastrophe?'

While he waited for his cheap laugh, in front of me Dr Conningem, Clare Short-haired Terrier, Robin Gnome and Margaret Bucket were nodding their heads off and, with their faces seeming to get closer and closer, began to chant 'Resign! Resign!' Behind me even my own so-called supporters seemed to be baying for my blood. The ministers I had chopped and the backbenchers I had not selected were in full cry joining in the 'Resign!' chorus. Even those I had promoted had it in for me because, to regenerate some respect for politicians, I had forbidden them to degrade themselves by appearing on radio programmes, live, at seven in the morning. I had not realised that they enjoyed being savaged on the *Today* programme. Either they were all masochists or so vain that they would endure anything for a few minutes' publicity.

What a madhouse! 'Order! Order!' Madam Speaker was bawling above the din and while, in the dominating context of the theme, I may have misheard, it sounded like 'Ordure! Ordure!', which I have always thought more fitting to describe the goings-on in the Chamber.

Sod them all! I thought. If this was how Premiers were treated they could keep the job and . . . I wanted out and decided to make a run for it. I had been told that in Parliament you need to be quick on your paws, and I was. I leapt on to the table almost to be seized by the Beast of Bolsover and, in the mêlée I knocked the mace on to the floor to shrieks from Madam Speaker, who left her chair and made a grab for me as I darted out of the Chamber, losing her wig and her balance as well as her dignity. 'Arrest that dog!' I heard her scream, her legs, which had once graced a chorus line, flaying indecorously in the air.

As I sped along those Victorian corridors of impotence, all that separated me from freedom and a fast scoot out of London and right out of political life was the Sergeant-at-Arms. Corporal punishment is bad enough but sergeant punishment is, presumably, one stripe more. However, the gentleman concerned happens to live at weekends in my village and is a friend of mine so he gallantly stood aside, pretending he had not seen me. Banking on not bumping into Black Rod, I raced towards Parliament Square only to be confronted by the biggest policeman I have ever seen. I was wondering whether to go quietly as his ham of a hand grabbed my collar when, thank dog, I woke up and found myself back in the peace and sanity of Church House, Kintbury!

What a relief! I was never so pleased to find myself at home but it had been a salutary fantasy which had explained why we get such poor political leaders and why they are bound to get progressively worse. No normal people – or dogs – in their right senses would take on the top posts even with the certainty of an overpaid, tax-free job in Brussels as a consolation prize for abject failure.

CHAPTER 4

The Heart of the Royal Matter

Ever since the Queen sent me a lovely letter about my book *One Dog and Her Man*, and especially since I was presented to her on her visit to our village in 1995 when she remarked 'Oh! That's Dido is it!' I have been intrigued by the activities of the whole royal family, both public and private – especially private. I confess to a prurient interest in low goings-on in high places – a habit acquired from humans – but I do not know what to believe when I hear people gossiping about them. The Chap hears one tale from pals who are close to various royals while his wife is told something different by hers, who are friendly with another set. This has been especially true of the long-lasting rumpus between the Prince and Princess of Wales in spite of their public admissions on *Panadrama* and other TV programmes. So I decided that I would use my investigative skills to sniff out the real cause of the rift.

As sources of information, courtiers have been notoriously unreliable down the centuries, grinding their own little axes to such an extent that, in the past, their heads often fell to a larger axe. Those surrounding the Prince are anxious to ensure that they retain their positions so that, when he becomes King, they will be among the socially elect and have nice jobs and titles. So they advise actions which they think will improve his popularity with the public, often quite stupidly in my view. He would have been far wiser adopting my policy when I am caught out: make yourself scarce and stay dumb. Above all never authorise anyone to explain on your behalf, whoever might offer to make himself a fortune in the process. Those supporting the Princess, who include her relatives and friends before marriage, are deeply disappointed at being out of the regal picture. So they take it out on the Prince by painting him as the cold, heartless cause of the rift, while Diana is projected as a warm-hearted woman wronged by an uncaring husband and is, consequently, racked by bulimia (although excessive appetite is something every Labrador has to cope with every day).

Clearly, if I was going to get to the heart of the matter – the real, basic cause of the break-up which has eluded all the self-styled royal watchers – what I needed was the evidence of truly independent witnesses, but where were they to be found? Obviously, neither the Prince nor the Princess falls into that category as both are far too emotionally involved, which also applies to other members of the royal family. The Palace staffs, from the top officials down to the domestic servants, must know a great deal but they are supposed to be bound by their secrecy requirements and it would be hard to be sure any transgressor was not taking sides. Then, while pondering the problem quietly on my beanbag, I realised that there is one impeccable group of witnesses, the genuine royal watchers who see everything from all angles and hear everything from all quarters: the household dogs.

Throughout the day, members of the royal family have dogs by their side. They take them everywhere – Windsor, Sandringham, Balmoral, Highgrove, even when visiting other people's homes. When they are walking, shooting, fishing or just gossiping, the dogs are there, seeing and above all hearing everything. Some dogs are even on the bed throughout the night!

Everyone tends to behave more naturally in front of their dogs than in front of people. Furthermore, with their extra perceptive powers, dogs can sense atmosphere and realise that something is amiss without a word being said, an icy silence being almost as eloquent as a row. So I decided that I would interview any of the royal dogs who would give me their ears and their dogjective views. Since many of the royal family's closest friends, including Camilla Barker Bones, have dogs, I would question them too. I would intrude myself as the joker in the various royal packs and then work it all up into the truly authoritative book on which I could secure a huge cash advance with publishers competing for the privilege of paying it, as there is nothing like royalty for generating royalties.

I had never met the Princess, which was a pity because I enjoy a hug and having my paw held, but before I began my inquiries my sympathies lay with her for several reasons. We are both females with the same nickname, Di, who had suddenly had to cope with fame when we were young. Like Diana after her engagement, I woke to find myself famous after the *Daily Mail* serialisation of my first book. We both know what it is to be hounded by the puparazzi and to have to pretend to hate media attention when, in fact, we love it. We both turn heads in the street – why do you think that reflex expression of male admiration is called a wolf whistle? – and people never tire of telling us that we are beautiful. We were both young mothers though, unlike the Princess who suffered from post-natal depression, I experienced only post-natal elation when my seven sharp-toothed, chocolate pups were weaned. We both know how to get our own way. I, too, can tuck my chin in, flutter my eyelids and look demure when it suits. We have both made our mark on television, though she did get rather more publicity than I did. But there the similarity ends. I am a country girl, all for peace, quiet and gentle exercise in the open air, while Diana likes noise, bright lights and dancing in nightclubs and pumping iron in a gymnasium.

I had met some of the royal dogs at places like Sandringham and Windsor when visiting gun-dog trials, and I could probably set up that kind of interview again, but for most of my subjects I would have to do what journalists call door-stepping, though that term is hardly appropriate in the sense that the steps leading to the front door of any of the royal homes are ever used for putting out the milk bottles or the cat. I could call it portal-stepping, though in fact I usually gained entry through less obvious doors such as the gate to the mews at the back of Buckingham Palace or by insinuating myself as a gun-dog into shoots at Sandringham and Balmoral.

As a seasoned writer who never reveals her sources, I am not prepared to say precisely which Labrador, which Jack Russell, which corgi or which dorgi told me what, where or when, but from such reliable witnesses I acquired the sad truth of the situation, including what the other royals really think about it. I can dogclose, for instance, that Charles now deeply regrets authorising the Wimpleby book which has done him irreparable damage, as even I, a so-called dumb animal, could have foreseen. Diana, on the other paw, regards her TV confessions as what French poodles would call a *succès fou.*

One needs luck on investigative ventures and my first slice was to find that nobody had ever thought of swearing the royal dogs to secrecy, so while some were diffident they were, at least, not bound by any legal constraint. From a few I got the ritual rebuff but it is surprising how haughty individuals who assure you that you are wasting your time because they will never bark a word eventually bark their heads off.

I found that most of the dogs were gratified that at last someone had thought of consulting them, especially as no public attention had been drawn to the fate of those of them most affected by the break-up. People tend to be unmindful of the trauma which dogs face in any unhappy marriage. Human nature, being what it is, ensures that the dogs get much of the backlash arising out of the irritation and frustration while the relationship is going on the rocks. Then they are bound to suffer severely when there is a break-up, with even their future home often being in doubt.

My most significant discovery, stressed by all the dogs I questioned, was that Princess Diana is not really a doggy person while the rest of the royal family are very doggy indeed. For most of them, a dog is an island of sanity in the sea of human folly which surrounds them. The devotion of the Queen and the Queen Mother to their corgis and dorgis is legendary, even though they have occasionally been bitten by them. As a shooting man, the Duke of Edinburgh knows the especial value of Labradors, while corgis may well have played a role in his long and happy relationship with the Queen because one should never underestimate the binding power of a dog. Indeed, many people meet through their dogs and, as one of the Queen Mum's corgis put it to me, 'Those whom dog has joined together let no man – or woman – put asunder!'

Prince Charles finds life intolerable without a dog nearby to touch and talk to, as the Chap learned when he sometimes shared weekends with him when staying at a country house to shoot. The royal black Labrador slept in his master's bedroom – on the bed I suspect – and the Prince was always out in the garden before breakfast giving him a run. At Highgrove, Balmoral or wherever, Charles is always accompanied by Labradors or Jack Russells showing that, for him, a house without a dog is just a building. Diana is rarely photographed with one, though she is often surrounded by bitches of another species. Furthermore, I was told that should a dog smudge her elegant and expensive clothing with a dirty paw the reaction was always brisk, to say the least, while Charles would just mutter some mild imprecation and forget it.

Obviously, there had been a crucial incompatibility from the start and the dogs had quickly realised that it boded ill for the long-term future of the relationship. Within two years the issue came to a crunch when Diana insisted that Charles should ban his favourite Labrador, Harvey, from the house. Admittedly the carpets were new, Harvey's paws were sometimes a bit muddy and he brought the odd bone into the house, but the dogs suspect that the real reason was that Charles was paying too much attention to him! Anyway, Harvey was banished and Charles had to rely for indoor canine friendship on little Jack Russells who are lively but lack the leavening influence of Labrador authority. The trouble with lap-dogs is that they are usually yap-dogs and Diana found them irritatingly yelpy. Though it may sound exaggerated, I have been assured by several sources that, from that moment, the fate of the marriage teetered in the yap of the dogs.

The universal truth which my researches exposed, and which all young people should note, is that very doggy and non-doggy people differ in so many other ways that it is, simply, unwise for them to marry. Genuinely doggy people tend to be more serious about life, as Charles is with his interests in painting, architecture, music, farming and conservation, apart from his high sense of duty in learning the business of government. Diana's interests, on the other hand, apart from her oddball concern for those with Aids, tend to be trivial and town-bound: fashion, health fads, pop music, dancing, smart restaurants and night spots, where she enjoys being seen and, especially, being photographed. All the dogs told me that because the Princess delights so much in drawing attention to herself, she makes sure that she is never pictured with a dog which might abstract some of the viewers' interest. In contrast, Charles prefers privacy when he can get it, almost invariably with a dog for comfort, and would not think of taking a walk without one. Conversationally he likes serious subjects while she prefers the psychobabble picked up from feminist 'therapists' which neither Charles nor the dogs could understand. She failed to see the most potent remedy of all, caninotherapy, though it was, literally, staring her in the face.

Such differences are bound to produce conflict and I learned, for instance, that it was the playing of tapes of pop stars like Phil Collie, which grated on Charles's ears as they did on the dogs', that caused another serious altercation. Any born Princess would have accepted the need to be staid in setting the standards which loyal subjects expect, but any commoner, especially one so young, would be bound to find constraints difficult to accept. While many people suffer from delusions of grandeur it was the realities of grandeur that bugged Diana when she found her life circumscribed by protocol and tradition, against which she inevitably rebelled by wandering about the London streets, for example, in scanty gym clothes and a baseball cap, though she only wore that back to front in the house.

While Charles, at thirty when he married in 1981, was widely experienced in many fields through his exceptionally active years in the Forces, and was well travelled and had met and talked with many of the world's leading figures, Diana, a giggly nineteen, was, understandably, immature and had also been poorly educated particularly, it seems, about the paramount importance of dogs in the maintenance of human relationships.

There were other important incompatibilities which did not go unnoticed by the household dogs. While Charles is keen on polo, Diana's real equestrian interest is as a clothes-horse. Polo, of course, is an expensive sport but not, it transpired, as expensive as being a fashion plate, which the Princess was determined to be, with irresistible encouragement from the media and the fashion trade. She certainly fitted that role, being as skeletal as any model and facially as beautiful as a young Labrador, which says it all, in my opinion.

It seems that, from the start, the various Labradors whom I consulted when I, literally, went to see a dog about a man – and about a woman – were deeply concerned about the different attitudes of the royal couple to country sports. There is a royal tradition of game-shooting prowess going back to Edward the Seventh with Labradors, in particular, being heavily involved. Prince Charles's great grandfather, King George the Fifth, was one of the finest shots of his generation, a difficult skill inherited by George the Sixth and Charles himself. The Queen does not wield a gun but her favourite sport is picking up shot game – pheasants, partridges and grouse – with a team of Labradors trained by my friend, Bill Meldrum, at the Queen's Kennels at Sandringham. If necessary she knocks them on the head, which is an act of mercy, though some of the media like to present it as cruelty. So, shooting is not just in the blue blood but is a part of the way of royal life in which Diana was not interested and to which she even objected. As the Labradors pointed out, it says much for the Prince's efforts to make the marriage work that he gave up shooting for quite a while, a sacrifice which only shooting people and shooting dogs can fully appreciate. Diana should have followed the Queen's example and made the effort to learn the art of 'picking up' pheasants with Labradors, as the Boss did so that she would not become a shooting widow.

Again, as the dogs confirmed, Diana also showed no interest whatever in salmon fishing which, as a fishing dog who can never get too much of it, I find hard to understand when one of the world's finest salmon rivers runs through the Balmoral estate and they even have a stretch of the Thames at Windsor, where salmon are beginning to run. This meant that fishing, which Charles loves, would also eat into the limited time when the couple could be together, with Diana having time on her own to become bored and incensed. With so few common interests, apart from their children, most of the dogs I questioned said that they had predicted the marriage could never work, though, of course, this was with houndsight.

Behind raised paws my canine sources also revealed that while Prince Charles behaves naturally, making no effort to hide any peculiarities, Diana is mistress of the demure, simpering look concealing her true nature, which is quite tough, assertive and unpredictable. While Charles likes a peaceful domestic life and detests rows, because they are so unsettling, Diana regularly threw wobblies – including her own body down the stairs at Sandringham – to draw attention to herself when, instead, she could have turned to a dog for support and sympathy. While it would be dangerous to sources to go into much detail, I can dogclose that she is far from the shy, badly treated, downtrodden lady as is widely portrayed. She has always been quite sparky and a Tartar with her tongue, her most hurtful remark being, 'I liked you better when you were a frog.' Normally Charles curbed any reply but, on that occasion, pursuing the fairy tale theme, he was driven to respond, 'And I liked you better when you were in a coma.' As one wise old royal dog was to tell me, it is words that wound, often more deeply than deeds. What is said, or shrieked, is often more damaging than what is done because harsh words can be burned into the brain when they are less likely to be forgotten or forgiven than some deed the memory of which fades.

Nor was the Princess backward at showing her anger and irritation by physical action during a domestic argument, which may have been one reason for all those workouts with dumb-bells. Neighbouring dogs at Kensington Palace informed me that it was common for one of them to remark 'Oh dear, the Waleses are at it again!' which must have made them sound like a couple of humpbacks having a barney. In fact they were astonished that the media never got wind of these noisy encounters, during which their dogs learned the literal meaning of the old phrase 'a right royal row'.

At competing for media attention Charles is invariably left in the starting blocks but, his dogs tell me, that is where he would usually prefer to be, especially during the present time when most of the media seem hell-bent on destroying any aspect of traditional authority for the sheer sake of doing so. Diana, on the other hand, could win an Olympic medal for manipulating the media, especially the photographers who always seem to be about when she is at her most photogenic in a black velvet cocktail dress or jade silk evening dress which, the dogs assured me, is rarely a coincidence. There have been many occasions when Charles could have denied some of the wilder assertions made by the media but his dogs say that, when tempted to do so, he took note of a wise remark made by his earthy ancestor, Charles the Second, when urged to take action against someone who had lampooned him: 'Methinks that to disturb a turd is to make it stink the more.' All dogs know this to be true and so does Charles, especially since the calamity of his authorised biography.

Incidentally, I established that the disagreements and incompatibilities on which the marriage finally foundered were not really due to any liaison at that time between the Prince and Camilla Barker Bones, a nice lady whom I met at shoots along with her husband, Andrew, who seemed very fond of her then. Media claims that there was an illicit affair at the time of the royal wedding and that it continued, thereby making the destruction of the marriage a certainty, are fallacious. Concerning the affair with Mrs Barker Bones after the collapse of the marriage I have been fortunate enough to speak to a Labrador who witnessed the telephone conversation which was recorded by a radio eavesdropper and then made public by newspapers. What happened was that the Prince was staying overnight for shooting at a country house where I have stayed myself. He went out after supper to walk his gun-dog, which was sleeping in his Range Rover, and then made a call to Mrs Barker Bones on the car telephone. Naturally the dog heard everything and he has assured me that the particularly nasty things in the tape recording were never said at all and must have been inserted by someone to spice it up. Charles's voice is so easy to imitate that comedians do it all the time. I have only the dog's word for this but, while intensely loyal, he is also a dog of honour and I believe him. In any case, the event was further evidence of the impact of dogs on human history.

I can also reveal that the Prince did not get Camilla's permission before admitting their affair, which was not very gentlemanly and made her housebound, which is horrid, as any dog knows. As for the affair between them before Charles's marriage, I traced a country-house spaniel who could have regaled me with many a spicy tale of musical bedrooms, but he had passed on, taking his secrets with him.

Since no dog was present I could not get the low down on the 'Squidgy tape', in which Diana featured, as she has since admitted, but another royal dog told me the truth about those silent calls made from Diana's telephones. They were made by one of the young Princes, William or Harry, having fun pressing the recall buttons. Though my source did not witness this he said it was common knowledge in royal circles and that Scotland Yard, which investigated the calls, was required to stay quiet about it. As for that kiss-and-tell Captain James Blewit (didn't he just!), who taught Diana to ride again because she had lost her nerve after a childhood fall from a pony, the lesson is clear – choose both your human and animal companions very carefully. Horsey people have a reputation for being suspect, but you can never fall off a dog.

While I will write my definitive book as dogjectively as possible, I have to admit that I was won over by the royal barkers' views and my sympathies have to lie with Charles for his sheer dogginess. Indeed, when he becomes King there is every possibility that artists will paint his portraits for posterity in the company of dogs, as the two previous King Charles were portrayed so often, emphasising the importance of dogs to the nation for all time, if only for helping to keep harassed monarchs on an even keel.

Happily, if there is a human gene for dogginess which Diana lacked, the two young Princes have clearly inherited it from their father. They could not be as keen on shooting as they are and not love dogs. They are also country-lovers so I trust that when their time comes to marry they will remember the recipe for marital bliss imparted to me by the royal dogs – marry a doggy girl!

Naturally, all the royal dogs were deeply worried by media suggestions that the Prince might not be able to function as King when the marriage ended in divorce, which seemed inevitable to them years before the human advisers realised it, because having a King and Queen who did not speak to each other would be ridiculous, especially on State occasions. The suggestions were dogswallop because, while a loving consort is a great help, royal life must continue like any other, as Queen Victoria found when she was widowed and had to make do with a hairy Scottish ghillie for her best friend, though nobody dared to write about that then or to suggest that they should write her memoirs. Anyway, thank dog, Charles will always have his Labradors and Jack Russells for comfort and they can be depended on to be faithful.

Like my Royal informants, I deeply regret that the marriage was doomed because of the dog factor and join with them in sincerely hoping that both former partners find future happiness and fulfilment. What should Diana's new title be? Her idea of 'Queen of Hearts' simply won't do, if only because it implies there is a knave lurking somewhere. Besides, Queen Elizabeth the Second already holds that title in the hearts of most people – and most dogs – after so many years of selfless service without benefit of excessive mascara or over-contrived publicity in operating theatres and clinics which has made the Princess look like a female Walter Mitty. I think 'Princess Mother' would fit the bill very nicely for Diana, but I suspect that she would not relish the aura of age attached to it.

Anyway, I have firmly decided on the title of my royal book: *Dogs' Honest Truth*. Watch this space, provided nobody slaps a D (for Dog) Notice on it! In any case, as the Chap has always advised me, come what may in the way of denials, threats or writs, I will stand by my story.

CHAPTER 5
Feeling the Strine

My Chap does not often reminisce about Fleet Street believing that there is no future in living in the past. Occasionally, however, people who want to talk to him about it come down to interview him, and I beat a retreat into the garden to do my own reminiscing, privately in reverie, without boring anybody.

It was on such an occasion that I received a long-distance telephone call from New York, which was not unusual in itself now that I have cracked the American market with my books, as I also have the German and Japanese. It was not an American voice that introduced itself, however, but one with an Australian twang: 'That you, Dido? Rupert Murdog here!' I recognised my caller as we had once met for a day in the shooting field years ago, when he seemed pleasant enough. The Chap had first met him in Australia long before he had become infamous over here, causing such havoc in Fleet Street that he was known as the Blizzard of Oz, especially among the unions which he really sorted out. Since then he had become an even bigger newspaper tycoon, with interests in television and Hollywood films as well. So, naturally, as an author as well as a private nose, I was intrigued to hear from him.

'What can I do for you, Mr Murdog?' I asked, trying to sound as though I received calls from such people all the time.

'Don't call me "Mister", Di. Just Rupe.'

'Right, Rupe. How can I help you?'

'I want you to edit one of my newspapers.'

'Great Scottie!' I exclaimed, 'but I haven't any intellectual qualifications for editing a paper.'

'You don't need any, sport, any more than you do for owning a newspaper, or fifty, for that matter.'

'Which paper do you want me to edit, the *Sun*?'

'No, *The Times*.'

'*The Times*!'

'Yeah. Let me explain my philosophy, Di. You know that we are in a fight-to-a-finish circulation war with the *Telegraph*. Well, we've cut the price of *The Times*, which means we're losing money on every paper we sell, and we still haven't got the readership we need. We can't make it a freebie – the first function of a newspaper is to sell – so there's only one thing to do and that is to take *The Times* downmarket and skim the readers off the bottom of the *Telegraph*, the *Independent* and any other so-called quality newspapers that might still be around.'

'But you can't take *The Times* downmarket without alienating all the existing readers,' I argued.

'I think we can,' Murdog replied, confidently. 'Never overestimate your readers, Di. You see I believe that most people who buy *The Times* do so for its snob appeal. They like to say they read it and to be seen reading it because it makes them feel and look superior. In fact, I think that quite a lot of them don't read it at all. They just like to be seen carrying it on railway platforms and walking to the office. I don't think it matters much to them what's in it and I think that going downmarket and bringing in the sort of stuff that's made the *Sun* such a sales success will bring in far more readers than we are likely to lose.'

'What makes you believe that?' I asked.

'Well, human nature is the same throughout every social class. Do you really think that it's only the lower classes that like pictures of tits? Upper- and middle-class men appreciate a good pair as well as anybody else and so do their women, who wish they had them and identify with them. "You want the best tits, we have them" – that should be the clarion call of *The Times*, not all this crap about being the historical record.'

'So, you mean you want to turn *The Times* effectively into a tabloid but keep it looking like a broadsheet.'

'You've got in one, Di! That's exactly it and I know it'll work. It'll make the paper more matey.'

'A *Times* in tune with the times,' I suggested.

'Absolutely! I can see that you're a great phrasemaker, Di.'

'But aren't you afraid that *The Times* will then just take readers from the *Sun*?'

'That won't matter because the *Sun*'s going after a whole new reader-ship, if you can call it that. We're going to take it still further downmarket.'

'Is that possible?' I asked, in my ingenuous way.

'It certainly is. I want to aim now at all those millions who never read at all including, of course, those who can't read even if they wanted to. We must keep pace with educational standards and they're going down fast so the market there is increasing all the time. I want to tap it before someone else does.'

'You mean tap what my Chap calls the boneheads?'

'Right! That's a good name for them but we can't use it in the papers. We want to capture the boneheads and the couch potatoes who only watch television. Have you ever realised that the paper with maximum read-ability would be one with nothing in it to read at all?'

I paused to absorb this wisdom.

'Anyway, the future of the *Sun* is another story which need not concern you,' Murdog continued.

'But why pick me for *The Times*?' I asked.

'I'll level with you, Di. I just knew that I couldn't find a human editor to take *The Times* downmarket. Even the yellowest British journalists are so stuck with tradition that they'd think it sacrilege and professional suicide. Nobody in journalism would ever talk to them again.'

'Then why not hire an Australian, cobb –?' I bit my tongue as I had fully realised it would be wise to avoid saying 'cobber', 'fair dinkum', 'tie me kangaroo down', or use any other 'strine' at such an early stage of our acquaintance. 'Surely any Aussie would love to cut *The Times* down to size,' I continued. 'It's the acme of pomdom. It's like taking the royal family downmarket.'

'They've already done that themselves, Di, and it's no bad thing,' Murdog remarked. 'But there has already been a big enough row about an Australian owning *The Times* without one editing it as well. No. I want you, Di, because, apart from having a great nose for news, you're not limited in any way. I don't suppose you even know what sacrilege is or give a damn if nobody in journalism talks to you again. I need someone prepared to do the unthinkable. On top of that, I like your style and critical approach to human foibles and you seem to be the most literate dog around. You will bring an altogether different kind of mind to bear on the problems. Once I had decided on a dog you were, obviously, the one.'

I did not disagree with any of that and felt so flattered that I did not reply.

'So, how about it, Di?' he pressed on. 'You can name your own price!'

I have to say that, snobbish as it may seem, the prospect of editing the historic Thunderer was unturndownable. Just imagine! I would be walking in the pawsteps of Lord Rees-Dogg and other great editors of *The Times*. As for taking it downmarket that was something original that I could get my teeth into and would be remembered for.

'But what about the existing editor?' I asked, not wishing to be responsible for putting on the dole someone I did not know and who might have a wife and family, as well as a dog.

'I am at liberty to dispense with any of my editors at the drop of a drover's hat,' Murdog replied.

'You mean a hat you can hang corks from to keep the flies off, like the one old Spycatcher wore on television?'

'The very same! And Crocodile Dundee! Actually I won't have to fire the editor. He'll quit as soon as he hears the new policy. Nothing personal, Di, but the record shows that no editor stays with the company when he has been ousted by a bitch.'

There was still one thing that was worrying me – the thought of having to work in Yapping or anywhere else in London, but Murdog quickly eliminated that problem.

'You can work from home. I suspect that most of my editors already do so half the time for they never seem to be in when I ring, not that I ever interfere, mind you. At least when they are at home they are less likely to get into trouble with bimbos, which is another good reason for choosing a dog. We'll set you up with faxes, videophones and computer links then all you have to do is generate ideas, fling 'em around and make sure that somebody acts on them. That's what I do and you can see that it works.'

'I thought that editing was very much a paws-on job,' I said.

'It is, but you don't have to be there in person. Look at me operating from America, though, as I said, I never interfere with the daily running of my papers.'

'So, I'll have a free paw?' I asked.

'Absolutely. As long as you take the paper downmarket, still call it *The Times* and leave the front page as it is. The rest you can tear apart.'

'You don't want the front page touched?'

'Of course not! We still want to keep the customers who like being seen carrying it around. You can spring as many surprises as you like inside.'

I did not argue as I had always dreamed of ordering 'Hold the front page . . .', and that was what he wanted me to do.

'Just one last thing, Rupe,' I said, sensing that he must have an urgent meeting for he seemed keen to end the conversation. 'What about the politics of the paper?'

'I wasn't going to mention that because I never interfere but, as you've asked me, I think we've gone too far to the left and are losing our readers as they get older and become more conservative, as everybody does once they have things to conserve. We need to switch back the other way a bit and I hear you're a right bitch.'

It was a statement that could have been better put but then, I told myself, he is an Australian and they are rather direct. He was correct, of course. There is nothing politically left about me or any other dog as none of us believes in fair shares or that crap about all pups being created equal, when it is so obvious that we are all different, as you are too. The whole prospect had set me alight and my brain seemed to be on fire with ideas.

'I've already generated a few ideas for surprises,' I said brightly.

'Great! But don't bother me with them. Just press on. Give the punters novelty. That's what people buy. You'll be hearing about contracts and suchlike by fax. Feel free to call me any time.'

I was about to hang up when he added, 'Just one more thing, Di. We must cut down on expenses – all these journalists claiming for taxis when they were really on buses, meals in expensive restaurants when they were really in snackbars and danger money when they were really in bed. The human editors say they have gone to the limit in cutting down but that's only because they want to keep their own expense accounts going. Working from home you will not need one and so you can go much further in cutting the others. By the way, as you'll be working in the outback, I'll send you a drover's hat to keep the flies off.'

I had never heard Kintbury called that before but I suppose he was right. There was a little laugh and then he signed off with 'G' day!'

I decided to give Murdog twenty-four hours to warn the rest of the staff about what was to happen and then I would wade in with my instructions, being determined to go the whole dog. To create an atmosphere of frantic action while operating from the quiet of my beanbag, and until the drover's hat arrived, I bought myself one of those green eyeshields.

The nub of the problem was clear: because of its nature, *The Times* had always been constrained by the facts and that was where the chopper would have to fall. Obviously, the first thing was to start a page three with sexy pictures, but they would have to be different from those in our sister-paper, the *Sun*. I felt that the idea I had in mind was quite brilliant, even though I say so myself. I called the pictures editor at Yapping to give him my orders.

'Surely, you're not suggesting page three frontals in *The Times*?' he said.

'No. Ours are going to be rearals – from the bottoms up. It's an angle nobody has properly tried yet and, from what I've overheard, there are just as many men in the upper classes who are turned on by bottoms as by bosoms, maybe more.'

I then explained how my idea would reinforce the readership of the *Sun* rather than abstract readers from it, which was a danger we had to avoid.

'We'll run a joint competition. Every week readers will have to match up the fronts in the *Sun* with the rears in *The Times*. The first correct solution to be opened will be the winner, with my decision being final. That way they'll have to buy both papers. We'll think about the prize later. Maybe a choice of a night out with one of the models, or even all six of 'em.'

'Brilliant, chief!' the picture editor replied, enthusiastically. 'As you can imagine, the more pictures we have the better. I'm pleased, but won't it be at the expense of news?'

'Sure, but what's the point of news?' I asked, realising that I was already subconsciously imitating Murdog's manner. 'It's all on TV the night before. Nobody gets his news from the papers these days.'

I could sense that I had made a friend of the picture editor who promised to keep me informed of the reaction to my appointment inside the Yapping office. He was not long in telling me, by fax, that the first response had been 'Oh God, not another recruit to the bitch pack!' which, perhaps, was understandable in what had been for so long a male-dominated profession. I didn't mind so long as I was accepted as the leader of the pack, as all previous *Times* editors have regarded themselves.

My next step was to establish a full-page gossip column with the fruitiest dirt, not just about Londoners but countrywide. It would feature daily items from my team of royal watchers, meaning people who generate spicy stories while interviewing themselves – or sometimes each other – in the bath. I would hire more of them and cut the number of windbag watchers, which is what the Chap calls Parliamentary correspondents. I decided to relegate the city page to the betting page in the sports section because the whole thing seems to me to be just a casino run by hoods, aptly named brokers, who always end up taking money from the suckers, just like bookmakers do. Furthermore, since the Maxwell scandal, the less that newspapers are openly associated with money deals the better for their image. I also started an astrology column for, although it is the oldest con in the world which would never fool a dog, millions believe it and who am I, or any other editor, to undermine cherished beliefs if it brings in readers. On the same page, which would all be aimed at the gullible, there would be lots of stuff about crackpot health fads, like aromatherapy and reflexology, as well as phoney diets and aphrodisiacs. I kept *The Times*'s once-famous letters page but made it more exciting, matey and controversial by organising the letters, not just by making some up each day but by ringing up people like the agents for pop stars and blockbuster authors who are always keen on free publicity and asking them to submit some. In general, in the paper, I would greatly extend the coverage of showbiz 'personalities', game show pre- senters and other non-entities whom so many people find interesting.

I decided in addition that I would slowly simplify the crossword puzzle so that the boast 'I regularly complete *The Times* crossword in half an hour' would be open to all. I would also initiate strip cartoons with the accent very much on the strip and with simple 'balloons' containing short words that all could understand. To please Murdog, who was obviously a fan of Crocodile Dundee, I would commission a strip cartoon on that theme but to avoid copyright problems and to site it in America, where Rupe is permanently based, while at the same time reminding him of his roots. I would call the hero Alligator Adelaide, alligators being present in the US where there are no crocodiles. At least one strip would be about a dog, modelled on me, to attract all the dog-lovers, and I might even stifle my deep personal prejudice and have one about a cat. As another service for dogdom I took the opportunity to bar any pejorative use of the word 'dog' in our pages, such terms as 'dog's breakfast', 'dog-eared' and 'dog-hearted', for instance. I was not blind to the fact that allowing such terms would make it too easy for the staff to be dumbly insolent to their editor in print. I had heard that critics on the other papers were already calling me the Dirty Dingo, which I resented because I haven't a drop of antipodean blood, and if ever there was a pomdog and proud of it, that's me. Nevertheless, I vowed to resist the temptation to publicise my own books unless, of course, I felt that it would also sell the newspaper.

My next task was to lay down a new set of dos-and-don'ts guidelines to be posted on the office bulletin board, which I was able to do after discussions with the Chap, who has long experience in such matters and was clearly hoping that I might get him on the payroll as a consultant.

[Doggetin No. 1]

From now on, except for page one, the silly season will last all the year round meaning that, as far as possible, stories will be trivial and, above all, will set people talking. Remember we are part of the entertainment industry, so pander to people's fantasies. They all have them.

As for politics, industry and such dull subjects, concentrate on scandals, real or imaginary. People love seeing the famous felled or, at least, brought down to their level, especially those in authority who, foolishly, expect respect. So, remember that no reputation is too great to murder and no character too splendid to be immune from assassination. Those who live by the word are fair game to perish by the word, so concentrate on politicians and any other loudmouths. For legal reasons choose soft targets whenever possible, meaning people who cannot sue for libel or are unlikely to do so. Senior members of the royal family, senior politicians and top civil servants are allergic to appearing in a witness box. Create lots of smoke and then exploit the common misbelief that there is no smoke without fire.

Think of the headline first then write the story to it. Comment is sacred while facts are expendable, so don't be afraid to make up news because that way it's bound to be exclusive. If we concoct a story that the other papers have failed to imagine, it is a scoop.

Really intriguing fabrications carry a further big advantage. All our rivals will waste time and effort trying to follow them up. Eventually they will be driven to abandon the quest or 'harden' our fabrication still further and then claim it as their own exclusive in later editions. We can then claim their copy as confirmation of our story.

Denials will only increase the publicity for the newspaper so the more vociferous they are the better. Always stand by your story however unlikely it is made to sound.

Never mention any other newspaper but encourage them to mention us. Use any means to get the paper attacked, especially in Parliament and on TV.

Try to produce stories about rows and fights. 'Splits' in political parties or boardrooms, real or imagined, always make good copy. If you can't find or think of any, predict them using the handy headline 'Row looms . . .' or 'Split looms . . .'

Crime, of course, speaks for itself. Britain has the world's best murders and the best spies, as well as the best political cock-ups, so concentrate on those.

Always get the words 'last night' into the opening paragraph whether it really applies or not. It makes us look busy and on the ball. Cover yourselves by making plentiful use of 'I understand that', 'I can reveal that', 'I am reliably informed that', 'it was disclosed' without saying who by, and 'sources say' when you haven't any.

The reaction to my radical changes in Parliament and elsewhere, including the other media, exceeded my expectations. MPs of all parties demanded judicial inquiries and bayed for Murdog's blood rather than mine. Quite rightly, it was the fiefdom of the Press, not the freedom of the Press, that they were on about. While the Tories, led by John Minor, who was still there, deplored the downward shift they said nothing about the shift to the right. Labour, led by Bambi Blare, deplored the shift to the right but dared not criticise the downward shift, because it was also being followed by Labour's paper, the *Daily Mirror*. The Liberal Democrats, led by Paddy Splashdown, condemned both shifts but did not know why. There was nothing that any of them could do about the changes as they all had to appear to support press freedom.

I heard nothing whatever from Murdog, who kept his word about not interfering and also about the present of the drover's hat, which arrived complete with hanging corks. He did not even respond when his favourite columnist Learned Bevin, grandson of the famous cloth-cap trade union leader, emulated the former editor by resigning. Bevin didn't like being squeezed off the feature page by Gob Beldof. Mastiff Paris was equally miffed at being out spaced by the Dulux dog whom I had commissioned to write a regular column on the hazards of being a famous caninity. His departure was soon followed by most of the other journalists who, I suspect, objected more to being subservient to a dog, especially a bitch, than to what was happening to the paper. Soon there were only the pictures people, a few sub-editors and me left on the editorial staff, but we managed to get the paper out without much noticeable difference simply by souping up the stories put out by the agencies and fabricating the rest.

Inevitably this meant more misprints but, remembering the Chap's advice that one should always turn adversity to advantage, I devised a clever little competition. We announced that the misprints were deliberate and offered a daily prize to the reader who found the funniest one.

Naturally we did deliberately insert a few that were open to coarse interpretation. This not only meant that customers really had to read the paper to find them but got it talked about, especially in pubs and in the City where some of the best were carried in people's wallets and shown around.

Through all these various changes sales rose rapidly, perhaps as much out of curiosity as anything else. This was very satisfying but I was beginning to feel the strain. Running a one-dog band from home was exciting but it made me man-tired by the end of the day. I greatly missed going fishing with the Chap but I was still enjoying the power I was wielding when I received an unexpected call from Murdog.

'Hi Di! How's life out there in the outback?'

'It's all going like you said it would. Sales are buoyant.'

'Yeah, you've done a great job. I think we've got the *Telegraph* on the run.'

I smiled with satisfaction.

'By the way, I really enjoy Alligator Adelaide,' Murdog continued. 'It made me feel so homesick that it's given me a new idea. I need a change of policy. You have done your job and gone as far as you can go. I now need someone with a different kind of mind and another approach to consolidate your achievements. I'm thinking of trying a kangaroo.'

'But you couldn't have anything more Australian!'

'That's true, but I'll give it a whirl.'

'You mean I'm fired?' I asked, in amazement.

'That's a word I never use, Di. I'd rather say "replaced". I wouldn't insult you by offering you any other job in the organisation after the editorship of *The Times*.'

I didn't know the Australian for 'crap' or I would have said it.

'When do I relinquish my post, then?' I asked, intent on retaining my canine dignity.

'You just have, Di. Good on yer!'

The line went dead. I threw my drover's hat to the floor and jumped on it with all four paws. I'd send it back and he could stuff it, corks and all. A kangaroo, indeed! A primitive marsupial that could probably do a boxing column but that would be its lot.

With Alligator Adelaide I had signed my own death warrant and the celebrations in Yapping at my departure had probably already started, but did they know what was coming to them? Or was it coming? Had I just been a fall-dog? My brain worked fast. Was the kangaroo just a joke? Had Murdog's real purpose been to use me to get rid of the staff and cut the expenses, which he had been unable to do any other way? Would he now, really, be making the retrograde step of appointing a new human editor who would recruit a smaller staff of his own choosing and then take the paper back upmarket? I never found out because the Chap rushed into the garden to wake me up as there was an urgent call from London for me on the real-life telephone. He said that it sounded as though it was from a certain Mr Collie Black, who was top dog at the *Daily Telegraph.*

CHAPTER 6
Tales from the Vienna Woods

I was surprised to find myself lying down on a couch which was far too hard and comfortless to be one of ours. I had heard about the casting couch, but hoped it wasn't that as I looked up and saw the bearded face of a little man with staring eyes, which were rather close together, a situation which, the Chap says, implies a mean brain. I looked beyond him to the wall where there was a large, framed diploma stating, in big type, that the degree of Doctor of Psychology had been awarded to Kurt Schnauzer, the rest being in very small type which I could not read. It was a shrink's couch, bare but for a hard pillow, and I had no idea why I was on it. Perhaps someone had decided that I needed treatment for the traumatic effects of the pressure of fame. All celebrities seem to need a shrink and what is the good of a shrink unless you consult him? Anyway, I was sure that someone must have brought me for I would never have gone to that man of my own accord. I knew it couldn't have been the Chap because he advises everyone to keep away from doctors of any sort, attributing his long life to this precaution.

Apart from the shrink's appearance his name rather put me off because the Schnauzer is not a breed of which I am particularly fond, though they have their admirers, especially on the Continent.

'Why am I here?' I asked.

'Because ve need to discuss your problems.'

'But I haven't any problems.'

'Dat's vot dey all say,' the doctor sneered, in his thick guttural accent. 'For a start, nobody can be named after such a famous royal personage as you are – Queen Dido – without developing grave inferiority feelings. I know vot I am talking about because I am in the direct line of the disciples of the great Dr Clement Freud.'

'Shouldn't it be Sigmund?' I suggested.

'Of course! It vos just a Freudian slip,' he grinned.

'Did you know him?' I asked. 'Sigmund I mean.'

'He vos before my time but I studied with one of his best pupils for many years in Wien – Vienna to you.'

Of course I knew what Wien meant, from the Wiener schnitzel, as there is little about food that ever escapes my or any other Labrador's attention.

The doctor poured two glasses of water and passed one to me while he loaded the other with scotch. I noticed that his hand was shaking as he took a swig and puffed his cheeks, as though it had been an urgent necessity.

'Now I vant you to take this,' he said, handing me a huge, pink pill.

'Vot is it?' I asked, unconsciously imitating his accent.

'It's a truth drug. Once you've taken it you'll have no option but to tell the whole truth about your childhood. The pup is father of the dog, you know.'

'What are you trying to find out?' I asked.

'Ve have reason to believe that you were gravely abused ven you were a pup.'

'Abused! But everyone has always been very kind to me, especially when I was a pup.'

'I mean sexually abused,' he said, with something of a leer.

'Sexually abused! But who by? I've never met my father and I left my mother when I was eight weeks old and have never seen her since.'

'Then it could only be your owner.'

'You don't mean the Chap?' I asked in astonishment.

'Exactly! Ve find that bestiality is as common as incest.'

What a thought!

'That wouldn't interest the Chap!' I protested. 'He's as square as Leicester Square.'

'Vich isn't very square is it?', the learned doctor replied, leaning forward as though he had scored a decisive point. 'Now swallow that pill,' he added, almost ferociously. 'Then, I promise you that you vill be amazed by what repressed memories you vill recall ven we dredge them out.'

I put the pill in my mouth and pretended to swallow it, being adept after years of practice at hiding a pill under my tongue, as many dog owners will have no difficulty in believing.

Schnauzer than began to examine my private parts, looking here and probing there as though he was enjoying it, which I certainly was not.

'Just as I thought,' he muttered while he made a note on his pad. 'Right,' he said, eventually. 'Just lie back for a few minutes and let the drug work while I make a telephone call to my partner.'

'For a second opinion?' I asked, brightly.

'No. He's a lawyer. If ve discover vot I expect, in view of what I have just seen by examining you, you'll be able to sue for compensation and you'll need his assistance. He could get you free legal aid.'

'Sue the Chap! He's my greatest pal. I could never do that!'

'You'll change your mind ven you realise vot ve have dug up from your old, repressed memories about the horrible things he's done to you. I guess he'll settle out of court rather than face the scandal. I'll have no option but to inform the police, you know, though perhaps ve could come to some alternative arrangement.'

'But I remember everything that's ever happened between us and if there had been any horrible things I would have blown them in my books to make them steamier and boost the sales. There simply haven't been any. You're wasting your time.'

'Dat's vot dey all think,' Schnauzer said. 'Now just relax for a few minutes.'

As he left the room I produced the pill from my mouth and dropped it into his whisky glass where it fizzed so furiously that I thought he might hear it through the open door. Fortunately he did not. He seemed to be talking about me and I heard remarks like 'Very promising' and 'There's lots of money there'. Thank God I didn't take that pill!

As soon as Schnauzer returned he finished the remainder of his whisky in one gulp and poured himself another.

'I have another partner whom you'll need to see, both before and after the legal encounter,' he said. 'He's an expert counsellor.'

'But I don't need a counsellor!'

'You vill – to get over the psychological trauma of accusing your Chap. And so vill he! Ve offer a full service.'

'Who pays for it all?' I asked.

'The taxpayers pay for the counsellor and for me and then the lawyer and I take a cut of the compensation. Right! Now let's get on with it. Keep your eyes closed and make your mind a blank. You are drifting into a deep sleep, a deeep, deeeep sleeeeep . . .'

As I pretended to be drugged he began asking all manner of crazy questions, making frantic notes even when I gave no answers.

'Ven your master tucks you up at night on your beanbag does he fondle your breasts and your private parts? Has he ever interfered with your anus?'

I answered all his questions, slowly and definitely, in the negative but could hear him scribbling away furiously and grunting, as though in satisfaction. Then I noticed that his speech began to slur and his pencil dropped to the floor. As he stood up, groggily, to pick it up I was off the couch in a flash, intent on making a run for it, but my curiosity made me look at his notes. He had written down all manner of false statements which I had never made accusing the Chap of indecent acts that could get him ten years in gaol. 'Right!' I thought, seeing an opportunity that was not to be missed.

I managed to direct him to the couch on which he was only too happy to lie down and then began to ply him with questions like those he had asked me.

'What happened when your father took you into the Vienna Woods?' I asked quietly.

His immediate response was to start singing 'Tar rar rar rar ra, tar ra, tar ra' to the tune of the Blue Danube, waving his arms in time with it.

'Ah yes, the Vienna Voods! Vot ve got up to in the Vienna Voods!'

'Did your father touch your private parts?' I asked.

'Oh, yes,' he answered with a seraphic smile. 'And how! And so did my mother! And my elder brothers! And especially my elder sisters! Vow!'

With his silly smile growing ever wider he then began to describe, in lurid detail, all manner of appalling acts of indecency committed by his closest relatives on him and on one another. They involved joint man-oeuvres I would never have thought possible which would certainly be beyond the capabilities of any gang of dogs, however athletic. There was also some suggestion that Satan and his imaginary minions were somehow involved. 'Poor devil!' I thought, meaning Old Nick as well as Schnauzer, as I looked at this pathetic figure and visualised his extraordinary family flailing around naked in the woods.

'What was your father's profession?' I asked, sensing there might be some diagnostic clue in the answer.

'He vos a politician.'

That was enough! No wonder he was such a mess. But then, one never knows with these foreigners. There might have been all sorts of other awful causes.

After a while, when the Mickey Fizz I had slipped him began to wear off, it slowly dawned on him that our roles had been reversed.

'Vot have I been saying?' he asked, as he sat up and rubbed his eyes.

'Plenty,' I answered, explaining how I had cunningly rung the changes. 'Just listen to this lot.'

As I began to read from my verbatim notes, his eyes got wider and wider, making them look even closer together.

'Mein Gott! I could never have said anything like that. It's all a pack of lies.'

'Dat's vot dey all say,' I responded. 'Let's see what the judge thinks. I am afraid that I will have no option but to report you to the Austrian police.'

'You can't do that,' he said. 'It would be ridiculous. I've never been to Austria.'

'Never been to Austria! What about all that extraordinary behaviour with your father, your mother and all your brothers and sisters in the Vienna Woods?'

'I've never seen the Vienna Woods and I only have one brother and no sisters. My name's really Bill Higginbottom and I was born in Bradford. The only place my father ever took me to was Roundhay Park in Leeds to sail my toy boat, and nothing could ever happen there. The place was always packed . . .'

'What about the Blue Danube?' I interrupted, still being suspicious.

'I suppose I was clutching at Strauss,' he replied, with a pitiful smile.

I could see that the truth drug was still working because his Austrian accent had disappeared and he was speaking in broad Yorkshire.

'Why do you call yourself Schnauzer?' I asked.

'What a bloody daft question! Who the hell would go to a shrink called Higginbottom?'

'And that framed diploma,' I ventured. 'Is that phoney too?'

'No. That's genuine. I bought it from an American university that churns them out at five hundred dollars a time. You could get one.'

'No thanks! Where did you learn all your patter?'

'I read it all up in the Bradford public library. Anyone could do it.'

I reminded him of the lawyer he had spoken to.

'Is he phoney too?' I asked.

'No, he's genuine. As genuine as any of them.'

Though I was beginning to feel that, in the circumstances, I might be prying too much, I could not restrain my curiosity about the counsellor and asked if he, too, was genuine.

'Of course! He's the brother I mentioned, Geordie.'

'Does he call himself Schnauzer too?'

'No. Higginbottom. It's a good folksy name for a counsellor. You know, down to earth. Sounds like the sort of chap who would give you sound advice. He does very well.'

I had often wondered what these counsellors did, especially as they now seem to be everywhere.

'What sort of people consult him? I asked.

'Oh, anyone and everyone who thinks they are suffering from stress. Butchers who get upset by the sight of so much blood. Turkey farmers who need bereavement counselling at Christmas. Hot-air balloonists who suffer from the continuous fear of heights. Even judges who get nightmares from sending villains to jail. The list is endless.'

I felt that I had pried enough into this peculiar family but, while the drug was still working, I could not resist asking, 'What evidence is there that your brother is fit to counsel anybody? I mean is he good at running his own life?'

'I suppose not,' the doctor answered, glumly. 'He's been divorced three times, bankrupted twice and served a prison sentence.' He paused and added, 'Frankly, he couldn't counsel a pussycat,' which I thought was putting it at its lowest.

'Then why do people go to him?'

'They are sent to him by the local authority or by doctors who want rid of their worst moaners for a bit and it gives the patients a day off and a chance of a gossip. These days the world's full of wimps who can't cope like their fathers did and convince themselves that they are heading for a nervous breakdown. Even gravediggers go for counselling if they dig up a human bone! What the hell do they expect to dig up?'

'But what does Geordie tell them?'

'Oh, a lot of crap about the value of shared experiences and the stress and strain of modern life which, in fact, was much tougher when we were kids and, at least, we sorted ourselves out. Then, if he can, he tells them to sue for compensation for hurt feelings and that's where I and my legal partner come in. It's the best scam in years.'

'But with your brother's terrible background how on earth did he get the job?'

The doctor shrugged.

'He just had some cards printed calling himself a counsellor and made up a good CV in case anyone ever asked for it.'

I shook my head in wonder.

'Was your father really a politician?' I asked.

'No, he was a bus conductor in Bradford when there were still white ones. My brother and I needed to better ourselves.'

He sat on the edge of the couch holding his head in his hands as though it were aching.

'By gum, this truth drug is bloody strong, isn't it,' he said.

I told him that I had decided against informing the Austrian police or any other, feeling that Schnauzer-Higginbottom would suffer enough having to live with his self-exposure, but there still remained one question which puzzled me.

'If all that fun and all those games you described never really happened, how were you able to recall it all in such detail?'

'Like everyone else I'm a sexual fantasist, I suppose. I just wish it had really happened and perhaps I hope that it will one day.'

I looked at him pityingly, thinking, 'Fat chance you've got, mate.'

'Well, I hope you are convinced that *I* am not a sexual fantasist,' I remarked, perhaps a trifle self-righteously, as I prepared to leave.

'Dat's vot dey all say,' he said, wearily, relapsing into his phoney accent, which made me wonder whether it was another Freudian sign that he intended to carry on with the pose that held such dangers for innocent patients and their families and for those who had to pay the compensation.

Later, when, out of curiosity, I checked with the street directory, I discovered that while Dr Kurt Schnauzer had disappeared from Harley Street a Dr Wolfgang Weimaraner had set up practice in Wimpole Street.

CHAPTER 7
Dog of Law

Sometimes, on a rare hot day, the Boss puts my big beanbag out in the sunshine to air it – 'blow the stink off' is how she so charmingly puts it – and I settle down on it, perhaps with a bone which is hardly guaranteed to improve the beanbag's scent, especially if it is one I have dug up after giving it time to mature. I don't know why but my beanbag, which is outsize anyway, looks even larger when it's outside on the lawn and I suppose that is what sent me into day-dreaming that I was on the biggest beanbag in the world – the Woolsack in the House of Lords, where the Lord Chancellor sits. Not only was I comfortably seated there but I was also wearing the Lord Chancellor's robes, his ludicrous wig, his chain of office and his even dafter three-cornered hat which I was required to don during my procession through the Victorian corridors to the Chamber. I was the Lord of the Lords and addressed as 'My Lord', even though I was female.

Sitting in front of me were the assorted peers, mostly life peers who turn up for the money though quite a few hereditary peers do the same if they happen to fall on hard times or have just backed the wrong horses. Most of them, of course, also use the place as a club because it is exclusive, has a free, central car park and the food and drink are cheap, subsidised by the taxpayer. Furthermore, unlike other clubs, there is no subscription and it is almost impossible to be expelled for you can still belong and use all its facilities even if you have served a prison sentence for fraud, which would result in expulsion from any other club.

Like all London clubs, the House of Lords is an excellent place to sleep after lunch, even, or perhaps especially, in the Debating Chamber, and some do it blatantly though they know they might be caught by the cameras when the proceedings are on television. Indeed, the Chap and the Boss have a game which involves scouring the TV screen as the camera moves around the Chamber for what they call the 'hibernators', some of whom they know personally. So I was soon calling the House the 'Hibernation Chamber', some of the members being hedgehogs who wake up occasionally if conditions improve, others dormice who sleep right through the session, come what may, unless it is a motion to increase the daily allowance. Sometimes I would drop a book or a heavy object just to see them all jump. Occasionally, though, on a hot afternoon, I must confess that I nodded off myself and found it made no difference whatever to the proceedings, provided I did not slip off the Woolsack which, like a lot of peers, is rather overstuffed.

The more I saw of the noble lords the more I thought that the honours system needed an overhaul or even elimination, some of them being clubbable in more ways than one. Peerages are too often awarded as consolation prizes for failed politicians and for people who need to be paid off for various services rendered, no matter how ineptly. The Kennel Club would never be party to any arrangement whereby undeserving bitches suddenly became ladies and quite horrible offspring become honourable, and entitled to be addressed as such, while some born to the distinction 'Your Grace' are a disgrace. It would have been very satisfying to sort the system out but other issues were far more pressing. Maybe all governments have found that to be the case, which is why honours have survived for so long in Britain, almost uniquely in the world, but I also suspect that Prime Ministers want to retain a comfortable place to go to when they are pushed out of Downing Street and they dare not deny their wives the consolation prize of being 'Your Ladyship'.

Frankly, being a glorified Speaker was something of a bore to an action dog like me, even with the comfort of the Woolsack, but what excited me was that I found I was not only Lord of the Lords but Overlord of the Law, responsible for the country's entire legal machinery, including the appointment of judges. Though revenge is purely a human attribute in which we civilised dogs do not indulge, I felt it was my dogly duty to do something to right the wrongs committed against my species by lawyers down the centuries. Such is the credulity of learned judges that they have solemnly tried dogs for witchcraft and sentenced them to horrible deaths. Thousands of other dogs have since been executed for other reasons while some of the most recent legislation against my species, while a little less absurd, nevertheless smacks of discrimination which would not be tolerated against any human race and would raise howls of political incorrectness. While Parliament steadfastly refuses to reintroduce capital punishment even for human serial killers, it recently condoned capital punishment for dogs which have committed no greater offence than merely to look as though they might be trouble. (On that score how many humans would qualify?)

My understandable antipathy to the legal system, and most of those in it, has been greatly intensified over the years by hearing the Chap banging on so much about its iniquities and the blatant money-grubbing behaviour of many lawyers. I therefore decided that I was not going to waste my opportunity to do something about both the system and the lawyers, for what is the point of power if you don't use it? Nor, with the ever-present risk of a reshuffle to make the unpopular government look different while still comprising the same buffoons, was I going to waste any time.

In our house in Kintbury, the horrors of the legal system are brilliantly summarised in a coloured cartoon drawn in the last century. It shows a cow, representing the legal system, with a scrawny plaintiff pulling on the horns and a half-starved defendant pulling at the tail. Milking the cow for all he is worth into his private pail is a bloated barrister and urging him on, with smiling approval and total support, is an even fatter, red-faced judge. Since those days, as is confirmed almost daily in the newspapers, the extent to which lawyers milk the system has steadily increased until their take from it has reached even more obscene proportions. In almost any legal action the big winners are the lawyers, battening on to the system like leeches, with costs out of all proportion to their contribution or intrinsic worth. Nobody can deny that lawyers' fees are the scandal of the age and it is no exaggeration to say that, in recent times, lawyers have probably done more than criminals to bring the law into disrepute, not just through their rapacity but in other ways. Some of them scour the newspapers looking for people who might be able to claim compensation for some alleged injury or abuse and then induce them to sue on the understanding that any money will be shared. In America some of them are called 'ambulance chasers' because they concentrate on people injured in car accidents, being tipped off by ambulance drivers who look out for likely cases, a practice sure to emigrate here, if it is not here already.

As I learned in our secret Cabinet meetings the rise in crime is the most worrying social problem in Britain for it has made all people fearful, not only for their possessions but their persons, and any political party which could really solve it would be sure of winning the next election. Many older people are afraid to leave their houses unattended and some have been driven to barricade themselves in at night, our own house, in a peaceful village, being like Fort Knox. Though fear of criminals has been reduced for some by our noble service as guard dogs we, ourselves, are at risk, not only from violence but from being dognapped. In our area alone, scores of dogs have been stolen for sale on what, in my case, would be the chocolate market. Because of my fame, the Chap is greatly concerned that I might be dognapped and held to ransom.

Having first declared this personal interest, it was not difficult to convince my Cabinet colleagues that anyone who could sort out the crime wave, or even looked like doing it instead of just talking about it, would win millions of votes for the Party. Nobody else had any new ideas for dealing with it mainly because any moves to get really tough with criminals come up against so many objections, not just from the so-called 'civil liberties' industry but from the government's legal advisers. So, when I offered to apply some dogjective sense to the law and order problem, provided I could be given a free paw, all my colleagues, and especially the Prime Minister, immediately agreed. With the government's popularity at rock bottom in the opinion polls, and a general election looming, they were clutching at any straw.

It was clear to me, approaching it with a mind uncluttered by respect for custom or tradition and without any constituents to worry about, that attempts to solve the problem just by taking the criminals out of society and locking them up had clearly failed. An additional approach was needed and I felt sure that I knew what to do, though I was not going to reveal my paw at that stage. As a dogjective observer which, by nature, no human being can ever be, it seemed to me that there were two components to the crime epidemic, the criminals and the lawyers, and that it is no good dealing with one without sorting out the other.

First, it was obvious to me that lawyers have a vested interest in keeping crime going and no incentive to reduce it. Criminals are their stock-in-trade and the last thing that lawyers want is for them to become an endangered species, which is what society would like. On the contrary, even if it is only subconscious, many lawyers must be in favour of an increase in crime because it has to be good for business. The more I thought about it the more did the linkage between criminals and lawyers seem to be the key to the solution, because it is the lawyers who prepare the criminals' ground rules for survival.

Many solicitors now regard it as their professional duty to prevent hardened criminals with dreadful records, including violence, from being effectively questioned by the police. They have a great deal of success and have no compunction or guilt feelings about ensuring that villains remain free to commit further crimes on the law-abiding members of the community. To another pack species, like we dogs, this seems nothing short of criminal itself, as well as unbelievably stupid. No canine pack-leader would permit it. What seems to me even worse is that when solicitors fail to prevent their criminal clients from going for trial, barristers then step in using devices which may be legal but to an observer like myself can only be described as crooked.

Before a case begins the lawyers defending a professional criminal, such as a burglar, armed robber, drug-pusher or even a murderer, try to force the police to reveal their sources of information, knowing that this is often impossible, and the case collapses. If the case does come to trial lawyers then try the gimmick of objecting to various members of the jury until they have twelve who are more likely to be on the criminal's side or, through obvious gullibility, be a pushover for a phoney argument. Once the defence of any hardened criminal begins it is almost always based on lies which the defending lawyers support or may even invent. Knowing that their clients are guilty, though professing not to do so, they do everything they can to undermine honest witnesses. They do this by making outrageous accusations against the witness's character usually prefaced with 'I put it to you that . . .' If the witness objects to being called a liar the lawyer claims: 'I am only putting it to you!' No witness is ever allowed to 'put' anything to the lawyer and, if he does, the judge, who is invariably a retired lawyer, will stop him. If it seems that a criminal is likely to be proved guilty his defence counsel will then hire a tame psychologist to try to explain how the defendant was not really to blame, having been abused by his parents at the age of two, and how a prison sentence would do the poor chap irretrievable mental injury.

Any serious argument between two dogs in a pack over property, territory or females would be taken seriously and settled quickly either by the leader or the dogs themselves. The difference in your world is that such arguments are not taken seriously but are treated as a game between two teams of lawyers who have no incentive to settle it quickly, rather to stretch it out for months, or years, to produce the biggest fees for themselves. Because of the costs, the law works in favour of those with the money to pay the lawyers and who can therefore stay the course the longest. If the law was not a monopoly and had to compete to get business it would have to be much quicker.

In short, the way that law is applied is not really about right or justice, meaning fairness, or about protecting the community, as it is in a dog pack. It is about the respective cunning of two opposing teams of lawyers who are prepared to use any technicality or trick to win and it is all done for money and for professional advancement.

One trick is to search old documents and books for cases in which some judge uttered a pronouncement which automatically made it what is called case law, and therefore eligible to be used as a precedent to settle modern cases to which it may have no sensible relevance. In our quarrels we would never be influenced by what some dreary old dog said a hundred years ago. Many of the outdated laws on which lawyers pounce are not repealed because Parliament cannot be bothered, usually being advised on such matters by other lawyers who don't like to see any nice little earner disappear.

If the prosecuting team gains a conviction the defence team will then do all it can to find a technical loophole which might secure an acquittal on appeal, a process which, of course, brings them all even fatter fees. This game, in which the judge, another lawyer, acts as a kind of umpire, frequently results in some of the worst criminals being returned to the community to continue their activities, which often involve violence. Such an outcome brings an additional bonanza for the lawyers, for the more often professional criminals get off the more likely they are to offend again and, therefore, to need lawyers, while so long as they are in prison they do not need them and cannot generate any fees. It is because the game is so lucrative and can be played far into old age, in the capacity of a judge, that so many of the country's best brains elect to play it. As a result of all this the law has become the first refuge of the scoundrel in more ways than one.

As I write, communities everywhere are being scourged by young criminals who cannot be dealt with effectively because the law does not permit it. They are allowed to steal, vandalise and commit violence without any deterrent punishment. As a mother of seven pups I made sure that when they misbehaved by canine standards they were quickly disciplined, and I would have regarded myself as derelict in my duties had I not done so. People may wonder why the human laws have not been quickly changed to cope with the yobbo youth problem. The government is advised on such matters by lawyers, and one answer may be that continuing the existing situation ensures that there is a healthy crop of young criminals coming along to provide plenty of work for lawyers in the future.

None of this makes any dog sense, and what I find particularly appalling is that a lawyer who is successful in doing such terrible things to the community is not only admired by his colleagues but even by the general public. Once, in a previous day-dream, I had been the foredog of a jury in the prosecution of a thug, known to the criminal fraternity as Crusher. His defending barrister raised so many doubts about his guilt by producing unsavoury witnesses to an alibi that I could not induce a majority to convict. It was only after Crusher had been acquitted that we learned about his previous record which showed that he had parasitised the community almost all his life with a string of convictions for very serious offences. When Crusher was released the court rang with loud applause and cheers from the public gallery, which was packed with other members of the criminal fraternity and their wives, who live on criminal earnings. Crusher left the court with a big smirk, but not as big as the one on the face of his barrister who knew that anyone who could get Crusher off would be much sought after by all the big criminals with plenty of money stashed away. We learned that the barrister was the head of a 'big criminal practice', which could hardly have been better named, in my view.

When I related this to the Chap he capped it with a real-life case he had attended in a journalistic capacity. A man, called Donald Hume, had murdered a car-dealer, cut the body up and dropped it in parts from an aeroplane over the North Sea. When arrested he had no option but to admit that he had dismembered and disposed of the body but claimed he had done it for three other men, for whom he invented ludicrous nicknames and a palpably absurd background story that would have made a dog laugh. His barrister was able to convince the judge that these people really existed. So the judge ordered the jury to return a verdict of Not Guilty on the murder charge and sentenced Hume to twelve years for being an accessory. The barrister was lauded to the skies for his brilliant advocacy.

When Hume was released after eight years he confessed to the murder and sold his story of how he had done it and bamboozled the court, with his lawyer's assistance, to the newspapers. The Chap met him and he said that he would do anything for money. Sure enough, when his newspaper money ran out he shot a bank manager in a raid, escaped to Switzerland and murdered a taxi-driver for which he received life imprisonment. It was this case which gave me my great idea for it seemed to me that the person most responsible for Hume's release and, in part, for his subsequent crimes, was his barrister. So why shouldn't lawyers be responsible for any calamitous results of their actions as doctors are, for instance? Or, to put it in canine terms, if someone deliberately let out a mad dog shouldn't those bitten by it be able to sue the person responsible? If the widow of the Swiss taxi-driver had been able to sue Hume's barrister it would certainly have made others think before sponsoring a fictitious story like that put forward on the murderer's behalf so successfully and with such tragic consequences.

It had been the judge who was so easily conned by the phoney argument and who had stopped the murder charge. Now, regularly in the newspapers, there are accounts of trials in which judges make other ludicrous decisions and pass hopelessly inadequate sentences. The appeal judges, in particular, seem to be searching meticulously for technicalities on which they can claim that convictions were unsafe and then quash sentences on crooks who can then legally claim not only to be innocent but entitled to massive compensation. In short, as in the medieval courts which had tried and sentenced dogs to death, there seemed to be another epidemic of Mad Judge Disease which urgently needed treatment.

Criminals were the concern of the police and the Home Secretary and there was nothing much I could do about them, but lawyers, especially the judges, were my pigeon and the more I thought about them and their ways the more I was determined to set about them. Nobody had ever dared to take them on because all previous Lord Chancellors had been lawyers and would have been regarded as traitors to their own profession. In my view the entire profession, from the most junior solicitor to the office of Lord Chief Justice, needed a flue-brush put through it and I had the courage to wield it. They would all have reason to remember Lord Dido of Kintbury!

It did not take long for my intentions to leak because my department was largely staffed by lawyers. The Attorney General, who, of course, was a barrister, warned me, in what seemed like a friendly way, against taking any drastic steps against his profession. 'They'll eat you alive,' he said. When it was clear that I intended to persist I soon learned that he had started calling me the Lord Chanceherarm.

But exactly how was I to proceed? I found that the legal profession was entrenched in the social structure like no other. While politicians are supposed to pass the laws they are drafted for them by lawyers. As a result, lawyers have seen to it that they are heavily protected by the law. They also have powerful professional bodies which fix scales of charges and are as ruthless and Jurassic as any old-style trade unions, especially against any attempts to break their monopoly. Nobody screams more loudly than the men in wigs against any suggestion that citizens driven desperate by criminals should take the law into their own hands.

The barristers have the Bar Council, so called because it wants to bar anybody else from doing barristers' work, as was shown by the way it fought against solicitors being able to plead in courts which was essentially an old-style demarcation dispute. The solicitors have the Claw Society, the reason for its name being obvious, which demonstrated its other purpose in its bitter battle to prevent anyone except solicitors from conveyancing properties.

The trouble with any attempt to reform the system is that all those in charge of it, from the Lord Chancellor downwards and including all the judges, have all been practising lawyers with an ingrained interest in keeping the methods and traditions of their profession unchanged. No lawyer brought up in the system can see it for what it really is. I was the first Lord Chancellor who was not and, therefore, had no legal axe to grind on lawyers' behalf.

While doing my research I had spotted an extraordinary anomaly which seems to have escaped the public's notice. Perjury – telling lies under oath in the witness box – is universally regarded as a serious crime as it threatens the whole legal process. Any criminal who lies in the witness box and is then proved guilty beyond any doubt has committed perjury, yet such defendants are never charged with it. Why not? The only possible answer is that the legal system works on the principle that it is legitimate to lie in self-defence, even under oath, and defendants are expected to do so. I would put a stop to that, or at least a brake on it, by making perjury an additional offence with a heavy sentence for committing it. So, if a criminal who had lied in the witness box was convicted on a charge which merited, say, only two years' imprisonment he could then be charged with perjury which would carry a heavier penalty. This would do far more than make criminals think twice before lying their heads off and induce more of them to plead guilty. It would make their lawyers think three times because my proposed legislation would make them open to a charge of being accessories to perjury, as so many of them undoubtedly are. So, in one simple move, the time which criminal trials take could be vastly reduced along with a substantial decrease in lawyers' fees which, for obvious reasons, are far smaller when criminals plead guilty and cases are quickly resolved.

At the same time I planned to make lawyers subject to prosecution as accessories when criminals whom they have been instrumental in releasing back into society commit further serious offences. My legislation would also make it possible for victims of such crimes to sue lawyers for damages. This would be a further disincentive to lawyers to promote phoney stories and alibis and to look for loopholes.

It seemed ludicrous to me that when criminals who had stolen money or goods are sent to prison their families are usually allowed to keep the proceeds on which they live in comfort until the villains are released to steal more. When a man lives on the immoral earnings of a woman he can be prosecuted. I proposed to make it an offence for any woman to live on the earnings of a crook, which are just as immoral.

As for the judges, it seemed to me that since they have all been lawyers and are likely to have indulged as a matter of cause in what to a dog seems sharp legal practices, they can never take a truly objective view. So I would disbar any lawyer from becoming a judge, for how can a man, or woman, who for years has defended people he or she knew to be guilty dispense justice and sit there moralising? It would never do in the dog world. In my new-broom system all judges would have to be lay people of proven professional repute and integrity who would have legal experts to assist them but, in passing sentences, would be guided essentially by common sense instead of written law, ancient or modern. I realised that this would outrage barristers who view judgeships as a lucrative way to end their careers with a fat, inflation-proof pension guaranteed.

All this might seem simplistic but that is what is needed. The trouble with the human law is that it has become far too complex and it needed an outsider like me to sort it out. On reflection, I suppose I should not have been surprised when the hate-mail started arriving even before my intentions had been put down on paper. In real life, I had never had anything but fan-mail and treats. The letters were couched as though from criminals who realised what my attack on the lawyers would do for them, but I soon saw where the truth really lay. They were so windily worded and larded with terms like *ipsi dixit* and *res ipsa loquitur* that they could only have come from lawyers. Were they from those in my own department? Where did their prime loyalty lie? With me or their profession? I had no doubt that the latter would always prevail.

It was not long before anonymous phone calls followed. At first when I heard the heavy breathing I thought it was some sex maniac wanting a cheap thrill after seeing a picture of me in my black stockings, but there was no mistaking the nature of the voice when it eventually chose to speak: 'Is that little Lord Chanceherarm? It's your *neck* your chancin' mate!' It sounded like Crusher, or somebody equally squalid, though it could have been one of those little 'civil liberty' squirts who find any restraint on criminals 'unacceptable'. Whoever it was, how had he learned my intimate nickname? And how had he got my private number? Some lawyer – or, maybe, all of them – in my office had to be leaking. I was never able to ask any of them outright because whenever I wanted any of my staff they always seemed to be in the library or at the Public Record Office searching in dusty books for something or other.

The next little threat came from the newspapers which had several nasty little items in gossip columns and elsewhere suggesting that I was corrupt or had a sleazy, hidden sex life. Of course, all newspapers employ lawyers in various capacities and some, I assumed, had friends in my department. I consoled myself that with such reactions I must be doing the right thing and that, in view of the ultimate service to the community, my personal feelings and safety were of small consequence. On second thoughts, however, I realised that if anything happened to me nobody else would have the courage or incentive to carry on with the campaign. I would have to take every precaution by having any treats analysed, opening any thick letters or packages carefully and regularly looking underneath both the Woolsack and my beanbag.

It was while going into the Chamber alone to make such a personal check that I found the ancient tome – an illuminated law-book of the thirteenth century, written in Latin and deliberately left open on the Woolsack at a certain page. Because of my difficulty with reading Latin, especially in that script, some kind soul had attached a computer-printed translation with a very modern plastic paper-clip. It marked an ancient pronouncement by Bishop Loin Cloth, one of my early predecessors, then known as 'justiciars', following the trial of one of his wolfhounds which had got loose in his deer forest, not far from Westminster Abbey, and had killed his best stag. The dog had been sentenced to be flayed alive before being hanged, drawn and quartered, and its skin had been made into a hair shirt which the incompetent dog-keeper had been forced to wear, hairy side in, for the rest of his life. It was this savagery that gave rise to the name Hide Park, which is the original spelling of that area. In addition to the wolfhound's horrible end, the Bishop, who was clearly a medieval nutter, had been so angry that he had also uttered foul imprecations and edicts against the entire canine species. One of these stated that no dog could ever be honoured in any way and any that was must be impeached, stripped of the honour and subjected to one hundred lashes by the public executioner.

It did not take me long to get the message. As this had never been repealed it could be used as case law to prove that it was illegal for me to be Lord Chancellor and, therefore, anything I did would be null and void. As I stood there, alone and suddenly feeling very vulnerable against the forces ranged against me – there is nothing a dog hates more than feeling isolated – I visualised the scene of my impeachment with the prosecuting barrister and presiding judge as that in our cow-milking cartoon. Every lawyer in the land would be looking on gleefully and none would be prepared to defend me, unless, of course, I offered a really enormous fee. False witnesses from the criminal community would be queueing up and, frankly, I would not expect much support from my Cabinet colleagues once I looked like being a loser. I would have been in good company with Sir Thomas More as a dog for all seasons, but I shuddered so much at the thought of one hundred lashes that it woke me up.

I still think my reforms are necessary and I set them on record here in the hope that someone will have the guts to take them up, though, dogjectively, I greatly doubt it.

CHAPTER 8
Dido the Maestro

On that unforgettable May evening I was sleeping peacefully on the back seat of the car with my head on the headrest, which the Chap mistakenly calls the armrest, and was surprised to see him open the door. Surely I had not been asleep that long! We were parked, like hundreds of others, outside the ancient church of St Nicolas in Newbury, where a big orchestral concert was being staged as part of the annual Music Festival. The place was packed with enthusiasts who had come from far and wide, including the patron, Her Royal Highness the Duchess of Kent, whom I admire very much for her gentleness, kindness and selfless dedication to her social duties. Normally, the Chap and the Boss, who was a Vice President of the Festival, would be inside for more than two hours, so what had happened? By the look of him he had something special on his mind and, whatever it was, it clearly involved me. He began to explain.

A telephone message had just been received saying that the conductor for the concert, an Austrian oddly enough called Willi Dogkovski, if I had heard correctly, had been taken ill on the way down with food poisoning or something. 'His players, the Vienna State Orchestra, are all here but there's no Willi,' the Chap said.

'Steak orchestra!' My ears pricked up immediately at the mere thought of a delicious Wiener schnitzel but the Chap, who has learned to read my thoughts, was scathing in his response: 'State, not steak, you ass! Your belly will be the end of you.' No other conductor was handy and, whether or not it was the coincidence of the Austrian's name that had given them the idea, they wanted me to take over.

'But that's ridiculous,' I objected as we were joined by the Festival's young Artistic Director, clearly in a state of near panic. Being trapped in the Chap's study for so many hours a day over the last six years I had been forced to listen to almost every major piece of music as he played his records or tuned in to Classic FM and tapped away at his word processor on my behalf, but to conduct them . . . and in front of the Duchess! I retreated further on to the back seat of the car, having learned to defy the laws of gravity by making myself so heavy that I am difficult to pull out, an accomplishment that most dog owners experience.

'You must help us out, Dido,' the Artistic Director pleaded. 'You are our only hope.'

I appreciated his position. He did not want to disappoint the audience but neither did he want to be forced to give them their money back when the players still had to be paid. Also, being new to the job, cancellation of a major concert would be a disastrous start for him.

'Why me?' I asked.

'Because it's your duty as a TV caninity and the most famous local character who happens to be immediately available. We just have no time to look for anybody else.'

Duty! What was that stuff? When the Chap has been asked to make a speech or do some other tedious task for no fee I have often heard him quote, wearily, 'I dreamed, and thought that life was beauty. I woke, and found that life was duty.'

'Yes,' the Chap said, increasing the pressure on me, *'noblesse oblige.'*

I did not know what that meant either, and duty or not I was not best pleased at being asked to make a fool of myself in front of so many people. It was bad for my image as a serious literary figure. I decided to plead total incapacity.

'Look here,' I said to the Artistic Director, 'I know so little about music that I was recently surprised to find that the composer of *Tosca* was not spelled Poochini, as I had always assumed.' I sensed that this admission of my ignorance had struck at his confidence so I larded it on, hopefully, with: 'My favourite pianist is Hamburger and my favourite singer is Kiri Te Kanameat.'

'Take no notice of her,' the Chap rapped. 'She's taking the mickey. She always knows more than she admits. All dogs do.'

There was, of course, much truth in that.

The two-man posse had been joined by the Boss, who was being equally insistent and pulling her rank, so the Chap reached in to clip my lead on and dragged me out. I have noticed, with humans, that it is never long before intellectual persuasion degenerates into brusque command.

'Come on!' he said. 'We'll have to move fast. The natives are getting restless.'

Indeed they were. The church door was open and I could hear the coughing rising to a crescendo. A slow handclap could be expected any minute, Duchess or no Duchess.

'But I can't read a note of music,' I said, plaintively.

'That doesn't matter,' the Chap replied, sharply. 'All you have to do is stand on the podium and wave your arms about. That's all any of them do. It's the players who read the notes. Just leave it all to them.'

'But I'm not even allowed inside the church,' I protested, playing my last card and always having been offended at being barred from the building.

'I'll fix it with the vicar,' the artistic director countered, briskly. 'The Anglican Church is nothing if not flexible,' he added, probably with the recent ordination of women in mind. How humans will bend their principles when it suits them never ceases to entertain me.

I was half dragged through a side door leading into the vestry where the vicar eyed me suspiciously as the artistic director explained my presence. Realising that I would need all possible assistance, both human and divine, I gave him one of my smiles. It seemed to work but had no effect on the rather fat leader of the Vienna State Orchestra, the first violinist, who was in a rare state of fuss. I could see what he would look like in his leather shorts, braces and green hat with badger bristles on it as he viewed me with increasing distaste.

Having been quietly told that a stand-in had been found, the players were tuning up, the noise sounding so like modern music that, at first, I thought they had begun without me. Perhaps a piece by Schönbone. Realising that my fate was sealed I resolved to apply my motto: 'When any task becomes inevitable lie back and enjoy it', though in this case it would be stand up. As in so many of my dreams I was on two legs, which is the Freudian result of a wish to be human, though I can't think why.

'What am I going to use for a baton?' I asked with female practicality.

'That's the spirit, Dido!' the Chap said, reassuringly, as the leader went off to look for one. 'I'm reminded of a song and dance which was popular when I was a soldier during the war. One line went, "You put your right leg out and you wave it all about". That's all you have to do, though make sure that it's the front leg. It's all any of them do.'

The Artistic Director backed him up.

'It's quite true, Dido. You don't have to be a professional to conduct an orchestra. They once had Ted Heath here and he was a great success. If a politician can do it so can you. Your charm will see you through.'

Knowing my susceptibility to compliments, the Chap also laid it on.

'Of course it will, Dido. There's nothing to it, really. The players never look at the conductor. Watch them on TV – they are too busy reading the music. So all you have to do is start each movement off and then look as though you are with them all at the finish. Then bow and make sure that you gesture to the orchestra to rise and take their share.'

Put that way it seemed easy enough.

Somebody had rustled up a white tie and started to fasten it round my neck but as I was wearing my best yellow collar I said that would have to do. I could see that it was going to be difficult enough for the audience to keep a straight face without having them laughing at my tie if went lopsided, as, I have noticed, the Chap's bow-ties are inclined to do. Anyway, even with some of the best orchestras, everything is very casual these days. Indeed at rehearsals they look like a football crowd which, perhaps, is not surprising as they share so many terms, like pitch, playing and score. I don't know what Beethoven would think if he could see them in their sweatshirts and trainers. Pathétique, I suppose.

A frantic search in the dressing-rooms had produced a large knitting needle with a knob on the end, withdrawn from a half-made cable-stitch jumper being knitted by one of the lady cellists on the bus drive down from London.

'Diss vill 'ave to do,' said the leader, handing me the needle knob-end first. I could see that he was horrified by the whole prospect but, like the rest of the players, did not want to risk being offered only half the fee if they didn't play.

'Right! Give me an A,' I said, as professionally as possible, while giving my baton a few practice swings to warm it up.

'Vatch out! Mind my eye!' the leader shouted. 'You don't need to be that athletic.'

The Artistic Director, stroking his beard artistically, gave me a brief rundown on the programme. It sounded not too bad. It began with Hündedämmerung – Night Falls on the Dogs – by Wagginger followed by Ravioli's Pavane pour une Infante Défunte – Dirge for a Dead Pup. The main piece was to be the Pastoral Symphony, which was the title that the Chap had chosen for his recent autobiography so I was certainly familiar with that because he never stops plugging it. I wanted a few changes to give the evening an even more canine emphasis. I suggested Chopin's Dog Valse, Opus 64, which is supposed to represent George Sand's dog running round and round after its own tail like George Sand (who was a woman) ran around after Chopin. Bach would have been appropriate, or even a piece by Teledogg, but what I wanted most was any one of the fine pieces which have been written about my great namesake Dido, the Queen of Carthage, and her steamy love affair with Aeneas. Even some modern music would have been helpful because, if anything went wrong, the audience would think it was part of the piece so long as it stayed cacophonous.

'It's too late to change the programme now,' the artistic director said, shaking his head emphatically.

'Q'vite so,' the Leader agreed, impatiently. 'Here are the scores.' He handed me a thick wad of printed sheets. 'I trust you can read them,' he added, rather sarcastically.

I brushed them aside, explaining that I always conducted without a score. I just had a gut feeling that a score would cause problems. I had noticed the instruction *molto allegro agitato* on one of them. I didn't know exactly what that meant but I was resolved to give them plenty of *agitato* peppered with *appassionato* for good measure and, perhaps, even a sprinkling of *staccato* while, like anything else to do with food, *'pizzacato'* sounded appropriate.

The Artistic Director then went on to the stage to announce, 'Your Royal Highness, my Lords, Ladies and Gentlemen, what would you like first, the bad news or the good news?'

Without waiting for a response he apologised for the absence of Willy Dogkovski and announced that Dido had volunteered to stand in, which was something of an exaggeration. As I was so well known in the area he felt there was no need to mention that I was a dog, or maybe he was too scared to do so. Those who did know were too entranced by the prospect to ask for their money back. Those who did not know did not want to display their ignorance and pretended to have heard of a conductor called Dido, nodding their silly heads, knowingly. Anyway, nobody dared leave before the Duchess and she stayed put, bless her, though possibly she was simply in a state of shock. Happily there were a few fans of mine present who had read my books and they clapped loudly, presumably on the principle that a dog that can write books can do anything, with which I am inclined to agree.

The fat leader went on to the stage to some applause and after a rather sheepish bow made a dreadful grimace to his pals in the orchestra to indicate that they had a nasty surprise coming to them. I felt that, had he been given the opportunity, he would have whispered 'Don't shoot the conductor, she's doing her best.'

'Go for it Dido, and good luck!' the Chap said, propelling me gently forwards. There were a few sniggers from the audience as I followed on to the platform and mounted the conductor's rostrum but most of them clapped politely, with their basic British instinct for fair play – Let the dog see the rabbit!, meaning give her a sporting chance. The Chap and the Boss, who had taken their seats near the front, had to be careful not to be seen clapping too loudly – a stupid convention in my opinion.

I realised that I was plumb in front of the altar and would have to restrain any inclination to be flippant. I rapped my baton imperiously and, with an authoritative wave, set the players off on Hündedämmerung. Having no score to occupy my attention I looked at them from time to time, making gestures to various sections, but not one of them looked at me, which I believe was normal practice. Indeed, I felt that I could have put up two toes at them and they would have taken no notice. They were all too busy trying to read their scores and getting their own digits in the right place to have the slightest interest in mine.

However, while I might not have been there so far as the players were concerned, I felt that I had the audience in the palm of my paw. Nobody even coughed, not even the Chap who always sucks mint humbugs to stop himself doing that, usually getting through a large bag in the course of a long concert. At one stage I turned round to the audience to see how I was doing and, as I had forgotten to stop beating time, it looked as though I was encouraging them to join in but, thankfully, it was not a vocal piece.

I managed to bring my baton to a halt with an authoritative flourish at just the right moment when the orchestra stopped playing and it brought the church down. There was wild applause and loud stamping though nobody dared to give one of those two-finger whistles in church. I had always thought it an odd human custom that any beautiful piece of music is invariably followed by that ugly noise called applause, yet I immediately realised that nothing sounds more pleasant to the performer.

I bowed low, being well practised in that art through my many appearances at the Inglewood Health Hydro in our village, where the Chap gives talks to captive audiences about my books and other activities. Having heard the spiel so many times I sleep through it but always wake up when the applause starts and do the bowing for both of us – a fair division of labour, I think. It was only when I turned round and motioned the players to rise that some of them realised they were being conducted by a dog. Their eyes popped, but not for long because, with the minimum pause – I was beginning to enjoy the feeling of absolute power over so many humans – I waved them off into the Pavane.

While waiting for the piece to end but still, of course, waving my baton, I had the opportunity to make a few observations. Because of his age, the Chap naturally meets quite a few mature ladies, usually widows, and I have often heard him say 'There's many a good tune played on an old fiddle', so I listened very carefully to the violins. I wondered how long the Frog horns would really be if they were unwound and what a pity it was they weren't because the players would have made quite an interesting sight coming on, especially if they got entangled. I was fascinated by the way the trombonists managed to miss the heads of the players in front, though sometimes only just. Of course the cornet is my favourite, the name evoking summer days waiting patiently for the Chap to give me the the end of his giant ice-cream. There was a very petite lady double-bass player in a rather short skirt who intrigued me. Every time she reached high up to play the low notes I noticed that all the men in the audience swung their gaze in her direction. It also occurred to me that for ladies who insist on playing the cello in skirts it would be more becoming if they played side-saddle.

After more furious applause, with the audience warming to me, we set off into the main item before the interval – the Pastoral Symphony, which has all sorts of lovely country sounds with which I am well acquainted, like cuckoos and drunken peasants enjoying themselves. Halfway through it I made my only serious mistake. During The Thunderstorm, when staging a ferocious down beat to indicate my command of the musical elements, the baton fell from my paw and, instead of ignoring it as a professional conductor like Mutt would have done, I instinctively bent down to fish for it. Nevertheless, since one should always turn adversity to advantage, it was then that my built-in advantage occurred to me. I continued to conduct with my tail displaying such virtuosity with that versatile organ that there was a swelling murmur of approval, so I continued in that mode until the end of the movement. I had forgotten the sanctity of the place but the show must always go on and I'm sure that God has a sense of humour.

During the interval I received congratulations all round, even from the Austrian leader, who now felt sure of his fee. There was still no sign of Willi, so when I was invited to continue I responded with 'I've started so I'll finish.' Somehow, word of what was happening had spread outside the church, which is on Newbury's main street, and people were offering ridiculous prices for seats while the media were demanding entry. I rather suspect that the artistic director was pleased with the situation, knowing that he was making musical history.

The first piece was called a Fantasia, and it was certainly that by the time I had finished with it. Inevitably, with a Viennese orchestra, the last piece was The Blue Danube and I love rivers, though the Chap says that he has seen the Danube many times and it is anything but blue. For good measure I repeated my tail trick, more positively in perfect waltz time and standing on my forepaws, so effectively that the audience could not resist applauding, even in the middle of the music. I thought I might have I made a bones but the orchestra was not fussed because when Willi conducts them in Vienna, especially on New Year's Day, he often encourages the audience to join in with clapping.

At the end I was given a standing ovation with cries of 'Maestro! Maestro!' (it should really have been Maestra!,) which I liked, and 'Roll over Rattle!', which I did not understand. It was considered most unusual at the Festival for a large orchestra to give an encore but the demand was so great that we had no alternative. Without one the audience would literally not have let us go by barricading us in the place. There were loud demands for particular pieces including a few waggish ones like 'Barkarole!' and 'Brahms for the love of Allah!' So, at my suggestion to the players, who by this time were completely won over to my leadership, sensing big TV performances and recording contracts, we obliged with the Canine Can-Can by Offenbark, composer of the Tails of Hoffdogg. It went down so well that ladies, young and old, were out in the aisles kicking their legs in the air and showing their knickers while being cheered on by the men, mainly the older ones, to the horror of the vicar who I could see was thinking 'I knew I shouldn't have let that dog in'. No doubt he would be expecting a rocket from his Bishop and would put all the blame on me. Fortunately my shoulders are broad, as is my beam according to the Boss, who is forever nagging the Chap for feeding me titbits. There was worse to come for the hapless parson when the audience encored the encore and the ladies really let themselves rip, figuratively speaking of course, though in a couple of cases literally when two went the whole hog and attempted to finish with the splits, which is strictly for professionals only.

When the din had died down I received a lovely bouquet from the Artistic Director. It is common practice in some countries to give flowers to men but in Britain this is regarded as effeminate. Being female it was OK for me, but I would have preferred something edible.

With some degree of order finally restored I was presented to the Duchess of Kent. It is so difficult to find anything to talk to royalty about but she helped me along, bemused as she was by the whole proceedings during which, of course, she had remained elegantly aloof. Perhaps I should have burst into tears and she would have given me a hug, like she once did to a lady loser at Wimbledon. If it had been the Duchess of York we could have talked about chocolates, apart from other matters which I had heard the Chap and Boss discussing.

In the heat of my success, while the adrenalin was still flowing, I had thought of throwing my baton for the crowd to fight over, like winning golfers do with balls and tennis stars do with their shirts, but I had caused more than enough mayhem with the can-can. Several husbands were still bawling their wives out for indecently exposing themselves, especially those of the two who had risked the splits with unfortunate consequences, both sartorial and anatomical. The weird convention that only they are permitted to view what we would regard as the public parts of their spouses is difficult for a dog to understand. Fortunately, for my relations with my own Chap, I had appreciated just in time the historic value of the baton. The Chap, no doubt, would already have been weighing up its potential value at a future sale of musical memorabilia.

Suddenly, the inevitable reaction came as the pressure was released and I felt so absolutely man-tired that all I wanted was to get home where I felt sure that, with the Chap and the Boss being so proud of me, there would be something special for me to eat. For my own safety I had to leave the hall by the back entrance, but I was still mobbed there by the media demanding interviews with their cameras flashing and horrible microphones poking at me from all angles. Having had enough of the media in previous dreams, I really did try to fob them off, but it is easier said than done, even though I was clutching my giant knitting needle, point first.

'Where do you go from here?' one asked, obviously referring to my future musical career.

'Home.' I answered with minimum response as I did not want to be misquoted.

'Can you tell us anything about your sex life?' a woman reporter from the *Sun* shouted.

'Dormant,' I replied. 'How's yours?'

That shut them all up on that score because they all had far more to hide than any of the people they wrote about, even including politicians.

'How much did they pay you?' another demanded, brashly.

Pay me? I hadn't thought of that, though no doubt the Chap had, the Labrador being worthy of her hire.

'That's private between me and my bank manager,' I said, rubbing in the fact that I was still the only dog with a bank account set up for my royalties.

I took offence when I thought I heard the epithet 'absolute bitch', but discovered that it was a critic from *The Times* asking me if I had absolute pitch.

Next day the inevitable headline appeared in the *Daily Express* in big black type – DOG PUTS WAG IN WAGNER, while the *Daily Mail* settled for the dead pan DIDO MAKES MUSIC, which was subject to misinterpretation. DIDO WOWS DUCHESS was favoured by the *Daily Telegraph* while several other organs cashed in on the royal connection. The biggest headline of all was in the *Newbury Weekly News* – ST NICOLAS IN CAN-CAN UPROAR – which, to those not conversant with the church concerned, must have conjured up visions of Santa Claus cavorting in a most untraditional manner. The more serious critics, some of whom had not been present, produced their usual gobbledepooch with phrases like 'a miracle of improvisation', 'made for fascinating listening', 'no-nonsense expertise', 'lyrical interpretation', 'avant-garde musicianship', 'a seamless flow of notes'. One cleverdick who wanted to air his knowledge, as most critics do, especially congratulated me on my *doglioso* rendering of the Pavane. It was a new one on me, the word, strangely enough, meaning sorrowful, which expresses my mood when I am left alone and can't sleep.

I was just reading an interesting comparison of myself with Jane Glover when the car door was opened and I was brought back to reality with a start as the Chap and the Boss got in. From their conversation it seemed that Willi Dogkovski had turned up after all but, while he had performed well, his impact had been nothing like mine, which had been unique in the history of dog.

As I dozed again during our short journey home I resolved that if I am ever asked to conduct in real life I will call myself something exotic. I mean, would Giuseppe Verdi carry the same charisma as Joe Green, which is how his name translates into English, or Monteverdi as Greenhill, or Casanova as Newhouse? I doubt it. I also recalled that there was a musician called Stokes who was so English that he had been born in London and died in Nether Wallop but changed his name to Stokowski, grew his hair long and made a fortune conducting in America. So I might try Didowski or, perhaps, Didonini, or even Doganini, as I am very partial to Italians through my long personal friendship with Lord and Lady Forte, though that, of course, is their real name.

All such matters will need careful consideration by my agent who, no doubt, will be the same individual as my minder and literary assistant – in other words the Chap. So all queries from impresarios and agencies regarding performances, appearances, contracts and offers of TV advertisements, bark-overs and suchlike to him please!

CHAPTER 9
Smelling Money

By nature I am a very happy dog, full of bounce and awareness of my good fortune yet, occasionally, for no reason I can see, except that I may have got off my beanbag on the wrong side, my thoughts tend to be a trifle morbid. On such a day I was beset with the irrational fear that if the Chap and the Boss were killed in a car crash I might suddenly be left unable to continue my literary career and would quickly become penniless. It seemed to me that I needed to get rich – and quickly – and, being a girl of action, fell to musing as to how I might do it. Writing another book seemed an unlikely route, and perhaps it was time I made some real money so I could give up writing altogether, if I wanted to, though the odds are that I wouldn't. We writers are addicts who expect our readers to fund our addiction. I know that, as with any other addictions, there would be severe withdrawal symptoms if ever I gave it up. Still, it would be nice to think that I had the option.

It was obvious that what I regard as the completely honest way of making a lot of money – by providing some genuine service to the community – would be far too slow. I could, for example, try my paw at doing bark-overs on commercial television advertisements but, though one is paid quite a lot of money for repeats if an ad is successful, it does not add up to a mint, which was what I needed. In any case, the way things have gone recently on TV I am too clean, too elegant, too well-spoken, too intelligent and too well-bred for current advertising trends which seem to prefer to feature people who are scruffy, coarse, ugly, ill-spoken, stupid-looking and, frankly, common. I suppose that the agencies argue that viewers, who are the potential customers, identify with this yob image, which is not much of a compliment should they ever think about it. Some of the advertisers go out of their way to hire little wimps to present their products, but perhaps there are more human runts around than I had appreciated. It is salutary, I suggest, to note that purveyors of pet foods, paint or toilet rolls never feature a scruffy, stupid or ill-bred dog nor do they ever pick runts. Furthermore, the dogs are never made to behave in a degrading, lunatic manner with their faces deformed by close-up camera shots deliberately made to intensify ugliness, as is the vogue with so many human actors in advertisements. However, appearing in dog food ads would not make me a quick fortune – probably nothing more than a free supply of the cans which the Chap provides anyway.

After only a little thought I was driven to the conclusion, cynical though it might be, that in order to acquire money in a hurry the thing to do is to exploit human gullibility and human greed, which are so often linked. Exactly how to do that was the 64,000 bone question.

I have met many rich people through the Chap, who seems to be the only pauper treading water in a sea of unsinkable self-made millionaires, and those who have made it with least effort are usually 'something in the City', meaning that they manipulate other people's money, with quite a lot of it sticking to their fingers in the process. Also, if I may say so without being unkind, most of them do not seem to be exceptionally endowed with grey matter so that avenue should not be closed to me on that account. Unfortunately, on close examination the City seemed to be little more than a glorified casino with stockbrokers, merchant bankers, insurance brokers, dealers in futures and the rest as the croupiers raking in other people's cash and rarely going broke themselves. I am not a gambler, which is what City people need to be, though they are touchy if one suggests that to them, and having already had more than my fair share of luck in life I decided that I was unlikely to have any there among people who seem more like wolves than bulls and bears. What the Chap leaves of my pittance from writing is too hard-earned to be risked in what seems to me to be Las Vegas in a cool climate.

Briefly, I considered becoming a desecrator, which is what I call a developer of country sites who buys land in a village, or a little town, fills it full of ugly houses and then moves to another area where he wrecks that before moving on again, but, apart from the fact that I just could not do such a thing to our glorious countryside and live with myself, I did not have enough ready money from my royalties to grease the right paws to secure planning permissions.

I have also met a number of tycoons – which, apparently, is a Japanese name for super-rich businessmen, or business persons as I should say these days. Unfortunately, the one who immediately came to mind was Robert Maxwell, the fat fraudster whom the Chap had known for many years, and I was allergic to being moulded in his image or that of anyone like him. So tycoonery was out without further consideration, especially as it would inevitably involve travelling to London for tedious meetings just to take part in a show of paws.

Fleetingly, the thought of the pensions robber recalled an exciting sequence which had once passed through my mind in a bone-dream when I had become the Dogmother of a vicious gang called the Wuffia, which lived off the proceeds from protection rackets. However, though I have the equipment in the form of powerful jaws and a daunting bark, physical violence of any kind is abhorrent to my nature and there is not much scope for protection rackets around Kintbury. What I needed was a gentler racket, though it would probably have to involve violence to the truth which, I have noticed, most humans practise without too much concern, to degrees that would cause most dogs to raise their eyebrows, if they had any.

Casting around, it seemed to me that the most fashionable scam producing rich reward with minimum effort was the compensation racket. Suddenly, it seems that whatever happens through natural mis-fortune, or even through crass stupidity by the person feigning to be injured, has to be someone else's fault for which compensation can be claimed from some quango of weird people who are empowered to award it. If someone has smoked himself into physical wreckage, tripped over a worn carpet while burgling a house, or injured himself while driving a stolen car which happened to have faulty brakes, each should be hugely rewarded at the expense of the community. Even if the misfortune is a dead baby, money is the balm that will soothe away the loss with more beer and cigarettes or a holiday on the Costa del Dole. These days, people can almost be seen sniffing the air for the fragrant smell of free cash.

Thinking along these lines which, as a matter of equity, should be open to a dog, a claim for so-called Repetitive Strain Injury seemed worth consideration but was not a runner for me, even if that condition really exists, because it would be the Chap who would get it as he is the one who works the word processor day in and day out on my behalf. I suppose that as my ghost-writer the Chap could sue me if he was so minded, but for him, as for me, it would be unthinkable to sue another member of the pack though that does not seem to put off some humans who are quite prepared to sue their parents to get money, even though it means the lawyers end up with a lot of it.

Then there was Battered Bitch Syndrome, which should attract rich pickings, but I am always in such good nick that I would not be a credible runner, even in the European courts where judges representing so many countries with historic reasons for revenge seem to take delight in slamming any British authority. 'Mental stress' is a more fertile field for human leadswingers because it need not show externally, being all in the mind, and, though we dogs suffer grievously from it when our motives for what looks like odd behaviour are misunderstood, I think it unlikely that any quango would be on our side. 'Hurt feelings', for which big money has been awarded, should be a more credible claim for they are something that immediately show in our faces when we are offended, as every dog-owner knows. I therefore gave some thought to sueing a particularly virulent book reviewer who upset me with a nasty comment on my first volume. These days, with the right lawyer and a sympathetic jury, I might have taken him to the cleaners but my publishers would not have approved, believing that any review is better than none.

'Sexual harassment', of course, is something that we bitches have to contend with all the time. I cannot walk down any street without atten-tion, which you would judge to be indecent, from any and every male dog who happens to get within sniffing distance – wolf whistles are not so named for nothing – but I am expected to take that, literally, in my stride. No quango would award me damages because they would regard such behaviour as 'natural' though it is equally natural in the human context, where males have precisely the same instincts. Furthermore, while I do not go out of my way to attract male attention, except when I am briefly in season twice a year, women go to great lengths to make themselves attractive to men all the time with provocative clothes, make-up, coiffures and alluring perfumes openly ad-vertised as being sexy. These days when some man responds and makes a pass he can be successfully sued and branded a pervert in the newspapers, which, frankly, is beyond canine understanding. Indeed, it would not surprise me to find that, having won heavy damages in a 'stress' case, an accuser can then sue again for the extra stress caused by the lawsuit.

It would also take far too long for me to join the Forces as a guard bitch and then get pregnant, perhaps by the chaplain's dog, and sue the Defence Ministry for false dismissal, which can bring huge sums to women, including some who are not even married. I could rely on the crackpot craze for political correctness to ensure that a big litter of pups, even one sired through a casual encounter in a country lane, should attract hefty damages but, frankly, I would find the process humiliating.

I am obviously too fit to claim radiation injury due to the fact that we live not very far from the nuclear weapons station at Aldermaston. Another possibility would be to link up, in a fifty-fifty deal, with some crook lawyer who specialises in ambulance chasing and get myself hurt in a trivial way which he could grossly exaggerate in front of the jury, but the risks of getting badly injured are too great for a thinking dog of my status.

A more promising solution is to sell something cheap and easy to make at vast profit, and the fields in which that seems to be easiest are women's beauty treatments and so-called 'alternative medicine'. I could concoct some phoney oil and claim all sorts of beautifying, healing or restorative properties for it, and it took me no more than a few minutes, reverie to come up with a likely winner. I would call it 'Dido's Oil' and claim, in cleverly worded advertisements in the glossy magazines, that it was made from the secret recipe used by Queen Dido, the beautiful and sexy Queen of Carthage. I could see the captions: 'The 3,000-year-old secret of Queen Dido's irresistible attraction rediscovered!' Then there would be a tale about the secret being deciphered from a clay tablet found buried in the ruins of Carthage, now in a bank vault. A brief mention of the Queen's love affairs would suggest that the oil also had aphrodisiac qualities, without quite saying so. In theory the oil would contain rare ingredients from the mysterious East but, in fact, it wouldn't matter what it was made from as long as it smelled reasonable and did no harm. Then it could safely be taken by mouth, a few drops every day, or rubbed into the skin. We could make it from mutton fat and sell it at a rip-off price indicating that, being so expensive, it must be especially good – a trick that has worked down the ages. Introducing extracts of 'herbs' would also help because 'herbs', which can mean any old harmless plants, are a money-spinning vogue these days.

Obviously, I would not be able to patent the product because the Patent Office would need to have the claims established, and might even demand to see the non-existent clay tablet, but I could trademark the name – 'Dido's Oil', or perhaps 'Queen Dido's Oil', or better still 'Queen Dido's Royal Oil', the word 'royal' always being a winner in any advertisement. It is amazing what you can get away with in an advertisement these days provided the claims are reasonably vague, and the Chap says that standards have slumped since his days as an advertising consultant when any claim that could not be substantiated would not be printed in a newspaper. The beauty editors, who are always desperate for something new to fill their columns, would be sure to plug my product, especially if I placed a few paid advertisements in their pages. Dido's Oil should sell like hot dog biscuits.

Then, of course, we could have the New Dido Diet to be published in books and serialised in newspapers and magazines, with lots of pictures of me looking slim and pretending to be bursting with energy. It would be based on some useless but harmless advice such as mixing bran with food to give it non-nutritious bulk, avoiding mixing biscuit and meat at all times or adding some quite unnecessary vitamin pill or mineral.

One simple way of cashing in on the alternative medicine craze would be to stick the word 'therapy' on the end of another word, like 'aromatherapy', 'aquatherapy', 'magnetotherapy' and the rest which have been invented. I could have gone for 'gustotherapy', exploiting the sense of taste, with the paying 'patient' lying on a couch sucking differently flavoured lozenges while being massaged and constantly assured that both the flavours and the massage are doing the whole system a world of good, but I had a much more promising idea.

In another flash of inspiration I invented an entirely new way of diagnosing and treating illnesses by massaging various parts of the tail. My advertising spiel would claim that 'New research by scientists has indicated that the various segments of the tail are intimately linked through nervous connections and other pathways with many of the vital organs of the body. So, massaging these segments in a special manner can alleviate and soothe away many kinds of aches, pains and other health problems in distant parts of the system.' The name for this new pseudo-science ought to be 'caudology', from the Latin for tail, but that would be too close to what it really was – codology. I would, therefore, call it 'caudex-ology', with the 'ex' referring to the non-existent reflex actions which I would claim were brought into play in tail massage. I would not earn enough doing tail massage myself but I could found a School of Caudexology where I could train other 'practitioners' to work for me. Dog lovers would, no doubt, bring their pets in droves to be treated, especially as it would also apply to cats, but that would be only the start before I tapped a much more lucrative market. Every human being has a little tail, called the coccyx, which is already alleged to be involved in the physical pleasure derived from sex, so human caudexology would have everything going for it. I can hear people, as well as dogs, saying in a superior manner, 'My caudexologist tells me . . .'

Another obvious field for exploiting human gullibility, which anyone can manipulate, as they have for thousands of years, is astrology, the crackpot theory that our daily lives are governed by the planets and stars under which we are alleged to have been born, and even by the moon. I have even heard it argued that because bits of a comet had crashed on to the planet Jupiter, hundreds of millions of miles away, the future lives of everyone on earth would be altered! No dog, however backward, could be induced to part with the smallest bone for a scrap of paper bearing a so-called 'horoscope', but millions of people who regard themselves as intelligent read them every day in newspapers or pay money to telephone astrological hotlines to hear some recorded claptrap. Even 'quality' newspapers have been driven to print horoscopes and astrology telephone numbers for fear of losing their readers. Nobody seems to ask themselves, as any intelligent dog would, 'If astrologers can foretell the future what are they doing eking out a living that way?' Briefly, I rather fancied myself wearing a conical cap covered with signs of the zodiac and poring over charts while plotting some nonsense which people would rush to buy, but I knew that with my sense of the ridiculous I would not be able to resist laughing in the faces of the idiots who believed it.

Ah well, I suppose that it will be back to the writing board after all, precarious as that profession is. So, I will press on with my royal book and maybe let my imagination rip and convert it into a blockbuster collar-ripper. There seems to be no limit to the human demand for prurience in any form and, while it would mean prostituting my art, lots of other bitches are exploiting it, raking in huge royalties, without much damage to their personal reputations.

C H A P T E R 1 0
Rank Outsider

One summer's day, for no good reason except that the Boss looked bored, the Chap announced that we would all go out to lunch and visit Stonehenge on the way, as it is only in the neighbouring county of Wiltshire. I had heard about the remarkable stone monument there and had seen it when passing in the car but paid it little attention, apart from noting that the big standing stones would have some appeal to the males of my species. With his inveterate curiosity and insatiable appetite for useless information the Chap had been interested in the original purpose of the ancient stones, their present one being to extract fees for British Heritage from tourists.

Some say that the structure was a prehistoric temple or a sanctuary where some pagan god or other was worshipped and sacrifices were made on an altar stone. That, apparently, is why the so-called New Age Travellers, whom the Chap calls New Age Scroungers, try to invade Stonehenge at certain times to celebrate some feast or other and are held away by the police at great public expense. Others claim to have proved that it was a gigantic astronomical device set up to provide primitive man with some kind of calendar because, at certain times, the sun shines through parts of it in special ways.

As we wandered around it I was certainly impressed by its size and the way the huge stones had been transported there – some from as far away as Wales. The whole complex is inside a circular ditch about a hundred yards in diameter and obviously dug by hand. Just inside there is a ring of holes for wooden posts. Then, right at the centre is a circle of huge so-called sarsen stones about a hundred feet in diameter. The stones are arranged in pairs each connected by a huge lintel stone. How the ancient Britons, if that is what they were, got them up there remains anyone's guess. Inside the outer circle is a ring of smaller stones, and others lie scattered about. The original main entrance to the complex is called the Avenue and is wide enough to have accommodated a big crowd of spectators entering or leaving the area.

The Chap and the Boss had visions of prehistoric men and women dancing around in skins and coloured blue by a dye called woad, though chocolate would surely have been more becoming if, perhaps, less frightening, assuming that was its intention, but my thoughts were on prehistoric dog. I had a gut feeling that the theories about the stones' purpose were hopelessly wrong and that somehow prehistoric dog had been involved, but it was only during a most vivid and exciting bone-dream on our return home after the visit that the extraordinary truth, of which I am now quite convinced, as I trust you will be, was revealed to me.

At the beginning of my reverie I was back in time, some 10,000 years ago, on that glorious and fateful day when the indissoluble union between man and dog was forged. 'Bliss was it in that dawn to be alive', as the canine poet Barksworth was to write in a different context many years later, when the hairy hand of primitive chap grasped the even hairier paw of dog in friendship and the spirit of mutual co-operation. Who had made the first approach will never be known for certain but I suppose it was the dog who was hanging round some lucky man's cave in the hope of being fed. Or the man may have deliberately lured the dog inside, being in need of warm and uncompromising companionship after some awful row with his prehistoric wife. In any event, it was a supreme moment in the whole history of both species, changing it for the better for all time. On material levels it put together man's eyes and dog's sense of smell and hearing on the one paw and coupled man's allegedly superior intelligence with dog's unquestionably superior speed on the other. From then on they were destined to hunt together and, in the case of me and the Chap, to fish together, though sheer companionship would always be the prime mutual reward.

Perhaps that glorious moment had occurred on the very spot where Stonehenge had eventually been built as a perpetual memorial to it *circa* 1500 BC, in the Bronze Age. Obviously it was constructed at enormous effort to be indestructible though, later, 'civilised' farmers would do their best to destroy it by using it as a quarry for building stone, being too idle to find it for themselves. My theory would certainly explain all the effort that had been put into it. Sadly, however, as the dream unfolded the true explanation proved to be far less romantic as, I suppose, knowing Man as I do, I should have expected.

Suddenly, in a shift of dream-time, I was looking at the structure soon after it had been completed. It was quite splendid and as different from what we see today as the Colosseum of Rome is from the original building since time and Man, especially Man, ravaged it. Seeing it in all its prehistoric glory there could be no doubt whatever about its function. It was the world's first stadium, from which all others including the one at Wembley are descended. It had been built by the local authority at public expense, and therefore with no expense spared, as a racing track for mammoths which explains its size and strength. The project failed because, typically, the planners had omitted to do the market research, including consulting the mammoths who refused to co-operate and with whom it was difficult to argue. They had tried other animals like pigs, which were far too slow and cumbrous, while the giant sloth was obviously a non-starter. Domesticated horses had not yet reached Britain and the various wagons and chariots in the vehicle parks at Stonehenge all depended on ox-power. In any case, the horse cannot be made to compete without a man on its back to supply the brains and that union was in nobody's mind when the stadium was in the planning stage.

A complete white mammoth from the start, the stadium had later been privatised and converted to a dog track. Why they had not thought of that first I will never understand because no other creature combines speed with such agility, intelligence, joy of running and the will to win. It was also used occasionally for games and even for open-air concerts, but dogracing was its prime function and it had widespread popularity throughout the Bronze and Iron Ages, so much so that 'gone to the dogs' became common parlance after being invented by wives seeing their cave-keeping money draining away. The ineffable joy of something for nothing has always been part of Man's nature, and his credulity in the form of betting goes right back to his Bronze Age roots. In 3,500 years punters have never learned that the bookies fix the odds so that, over any season, they are bound to win. Instead, punters remain deluded that the odds will somehow work in their favour and never seem to ask why bookmakers are always rich, any more than they did on my memorable day at the Stonehenge Stadium.

As for the religious theory, the only deities that were worshipped there were the goddess Fortune and the god of bookmakers, Bacchus. As for being an astronomical apparatus, the only calendar with which it was associated was the racing calendar, the only dates being with the dogs! The Bronze Age was only ushered in because the alloy was needed to make the pennies, then a sizeable sum, to put on the dogs. Furthermore, it was no coincidence that the site chosen for the stadium was built on chalk for it meant that there was plenty on hand for the bookies to mark up the odds, which they did with large stripes on the sides of the stones facing the spectators. This early use of chalk may well have been the origin of mathematics and writing in Britain because the bookies soon had to invent numbers. It was simply not feasible to chalk up two hundred stripes for an outsider.

The wooden posts which had fitted in the outside ring of holes and have puzzled archaeologists for so long were part of the seating arrangements, including the boxes for the nobs and the royal box, with the ordinary prehistoric punters having to stand, as usual. It was impossible to enter the closely guarded royal enclosure without a wooden ticket, paper not having been invented, and once inside it was obligatory for the men to wear a most uncomfortable cylindrical hat made from sections sawn from the marrowbone of a mammoth's leg. They were forbidden to remove it, however hot the day, except when any royals arrived in their ox-drawn chariots, when they had to wave it as a mark of respect. The women could wear any kind of hat they liked so long as they were all different, any two found wearing the same hat being ostracised for the season. This strange practice quickly led to the production of outrageous hats at even more outrageous prices by hatters who developed the reputation for being mad though, to an objective onlooker like myself, it was the women who were mad to wear them and the men who were even madder to pay for them. The bookies had a theory that the bigger the hat worn by a woman punter the smaller the brain beneath it and, therefore, the less chance she would have of being able to spot a winner – a belief which, I am told, persists to this day.

So this was the hallowed heath where the first bookies had taken bets, paid out and sometimes welshed; the first tipsters had tipped; where the first touts had touted; the first tic-tac men had tic-taced; from which the first trainers had been warned off and the first race gangs had gathered with violent intent.

Some of the races were on the flat consisting of one or more circuits round the outside ring while others were 'over the stones' – small ones, some of which can still be seen lying around. But by far the most important and easily the most popular were the slalom races in which the runners had to wind their way in and out of the gaps between the standing stones. Regularly at Cruft's, and shows elsewhere, we demonstrate how clever we are at slaloms. It's dyed in the genes since Stonehenge days because those who were best at it were chosen for breeding.

At Stonehenge, however, slaloms were much more difficult and dangerous than it would appear today because of the fiendish cunning of the course constructor, Rockcake, an early ancestor of my Hickstead friend Douglas Bunn, a name which has since generated happy associations on more counts than one, but which, on that day, spelled horrendous near-disaster. It was Rockcake's habit to pack the slalom gaps with sharp, cutting flints and even the edges of the standing stones were sharpened up, though they have since weathered smooth over the centuries. Small wonder that these narrow hazards had names like the Scraper, the Slasher, the Squeezer, the Crusher and the Flayer. Unlike a modern slalom the dogs could not be timed individually over the course because stopwatches had not been invented, so they all raced together. Having to squeeze through the razor-sharp gaps at speed with all the other dogs pressing on, and with no fouls barred, caused fearful injuries but the spectators enjoyed that in those days, rather like some still do at motor races.

Scars became a badge of distinction for the truly professional dogs, like those scars of honour that Germans used to have on their faces after sabre duels, and consistent winners were held in the highest respect. The most famous dog up to that time had been known to all the punters as Wilt the Tilt because of the peculiar but highly successful angle at which he attacked the slalom gaps. In a long and brilliant racing career he won all the classics, was never up before the stewards and, when he retired to stud, the whole county was named after him. (The canine origin of my own county, which was originally spelled Barkshire, as it is still pronounced, is too obvious for comment: the neighbouring county of Oxfordshire – Oxon for short – commemoraties a clumsier and far less intelligent creature.) Wilt the Tilt had been able to charge enormous stud fees paid in the currency of the day – bronze coins, cattle, wives, daughters or weapons. He died a very rich dog.

Races were in progress that day, in my dream, with Queen Didoicea in the royal box, racing having been the sport of queens before it became the sport of kings. She was a fierce-looking, sturdily built female wearing the skin of a woolly rhinoceros, which suited her complexion. Her body was heavily stained with woad which she had even applied to her hair, thereby inventing the first blue rinse. Naturally all the other upper-class women followed her fashion and the royal meetings could be aptly described as antique woad shows.

The meeting was regarded as officially open once Didoicea had arrived in her ox-chariot. She waved imperiously to the crowd who were encouraged to cheer but discouraged from becoming too familiar by the razor-sharp bronze scythes fixed to the chariot wheels, the penalty for such presumption being 'off with their legs'. Though scythes have now been abandoned, the wave of her hand was to become traditional and the Queen continues it to this day. Didoicea could be charming if it suited but was unpredictable unless she was irritated, when her behaviour could be predicted with certainty. In particular, it was rumoured, she would have the guts of any dog that lost a race for garters if she happened to have backed it.

As you can imagine I was not best pleased – indeed I was very frightened – when, after watching a couple of races with injured dogs being carried off half flayed, my name was called among the starters in the main race of the day, the classic Amesbury Cup, presumably by some wag who had put it forward as a joke. It was a winner-takes-all race and, as a dog that had come from nowhere up against the best and most experienced in the land, including some of Wilt's progeny, the odds against me were a hundred to one.

There was no escape. Not only was I hemmed in by the huge club-carrying crowd, fearsome in their skins, but Labrador honour was at stake. As I surveyed the opposition when we all paraded in the paddock – the smaller circle in the centre – I could see that they were a rascally-looking lot who would, no doubt, be up to every trick in the book with bumping, boring and occasional biting being second nature to them. Genetically they were rubbish and unrecognisable as breeds, the Kennel Club not having been invented either. The only feature they were likely to have in common was to be bad and resentful losers. I was the only filly in the race but could expect no quarter for, in those days, even the human wives were apt to be clubbed on the head if they talked or acted out of turn. I reassured myself by recalling that breeding should count and I was the only thoroughbred among them. Also, using my superior intelligence, I realised that my best ploy to avoid being nobbled was to get out in front immediately while the professionals would, no doubt, be pacing themselves. I would then keep well away from the rest of the field hoping that I could hold my lead or, if exhausted, pull up with some spurious injury, trusting that the Queen might forgive me for a good try.

The odds-on favourite was a huge cross between a mastiff and a bull terrier called Caradog, after which some famous human Celt would later be named. He had won many races and regarded himself as the Wilt the Tilt of his day. He was wearing a spiky collar which was illegal, but nobody dared tell him so. The second favourite, and bitter rival of Caradog, was a horrible-looking ginger lurcher of wild, Scottish origin called Jock Strapp. Only the race would show who was the nastier piece of work.

The bodies of all the runners were badly scarred by previous races and, naturally, this increased my concern as I paraded around because it is so important that I remain presentable, with two ears and a whole tail, when I appear on television or open fairs and fêtes. Jock Strapp's tail had been severely docked during an encounter with Caradog in the Slasher some weeks earlier, and I noticed a dark gentleman jigging his way from a hut with many windows, called the Totem, and quietly singing, 'I bet mah money on de bob-tailed dog, do-dah, do-dah . . .'

In the paddock Julius Wilson, after whom Caesar would later be named because their ears were similar, was sizing up our form.

'Dido has to be the dark dog in the race,' he told his listeners, 'because she has no form whatever and apparently no trainer from whom I could get anything "straight from the dog's mouth". The market is giving two hundred to one against her but we can't entirely rule her out,' he added, as tipsters do to cover themselves.

Soon we were under starter's orders. The starting skin had been made from some hapless beast, tape not having been invented, while the starter wore a black earthenware bowl on his head from which the modern bowler is derived. He also carried a flag stained red with blood which he waved frantically whenever there was a false start or if some dog which the Queen was known to have backed got away to a bad start, whereupon the race was declared void and restarted. The commentator was Petroc O'Sullivan from Ireland where the natives, in the bogs there, have always been so mad on betting that to this very day they call their pounds 'punts' and those who stake them 'punters'.

The going was hard which suited my race plan for a quick get away and, while the professionals hung back to conserve their energy for the long race as I had anticipated, I was soon many yards in front.

'Oh dear, Dido has taken off far too fast', Petroc cried in his unmistakable voice. 'She'll never be able to complete three circuits of this punishing course at that pace.'

'Won't I indeed!' I thought. They don't know what breeding can do for a dog. There was no way I would let Labradors down, and the thought of being the Queen's garters kept me going anyway.

There was a cheer from all the bookies as Petroc screamed, 'Caradog has stuck in a gap. He can't get out for his spiky collar. What a turn up for the book! Jock Strapp has fallen behind and is sportingly trying to free Caradog. No he's not. He's got Caradog by the ar-, sorry, the rear end, and is settling a few old scores. Bacchus help him when Caradog gets free!'

What Jock Strapp was doing, confident he could make up the lost ground, was not only to get his revenge for his lost tail but to put Caradog out of contention in the Championship List for the rest of the season.

'Dido has increased her lead but I think it's academic – she can't possibly keep going,' Petroc shouted.

'Come on Dido!' the Queen, who had been silent, suddenly bellowed in a voice so deep that it would have raised eyebrows today and suspicions that she was a prehistoric man in drag but, apparently, it was common to the women of the time, as I realised when the women-in-waiting began to cheer me on even though they hadn't backed me, in order to curry favour with the Queen.

There was a sigh of sadness from the crowd as, immediately, most of the dogs which they had backed slackened their pace to preserve their own skins because they were only too aware that any runner that beat the dog backed by the Queen was likely to be up before the stewards, disqualified on some pretext, suspended and then severely 'disciplined'. Though taking my time going through the dangerous gaps I looked like winning in a canter, but having done his dirty work Jock Strapp, still dripping blood, wanted to be second and to show the crowd that he could win if he liked.

'Jock Strapp is coming up fast on the granite rails,' Petroc shouted, trying to keep the excitement going though everybody knew I was now a racing certainty.

I glanced backwards to see Jock Strapp hard on my tail with a hideous look on his face, clearly intending to give me a dreadful slash with his fangs if he could get away with it.

'They're almost neck and neck coming up to Flattenem Corner for the third time,' Petroc screamed.

This was the most dangerous hazard of all, packed with razor-edged flints, and I negotiated it most carefully while Jock Strapp, in a desperate bid to overhaul me, suddenly wished he had been wearing that item of protective clothing with which his name has forever been associated since. For some reason I did not understand at the time, but which the Chap has since explained, his howl suddenly became two octaves higher and he retired from the race with his forepaws as well as his tail between his legs.

Once into the straight which, in fact, was still curved, it was a doddle and I passed the winning post where the starter, who was also the judge, doffed his pot-bowler and waved a chequered flag. I did a lap of honour round the course, to loud boos from all who had backed the favourites, but I was the bookies' darling and they all chaired me towards the royal box for the presentation, which would be regarded as most irregular today.

There was a further, and I think fairer, difference from modern practice. As there were no owners in those days it was the winning dogs who received the trophies. These days, owners or their wives, both dolled up to the nines, pose for the cameras with racing trophies and fat cheques for which they have done nothing except put up money. All race-goers talk about 'going racing' when all they are doing is watching other creatures race and, of course, eat and drink, especially the latter.

Several of the bookies were carrying heavy skin bags and, on reaching the royal box, the first thing they did was to hand them over with a low bow because they contained the Queen's winnings in bronze coins with her rather repulsive head on them. (I doubt that the bookies bring our Queen her winnings and imagine that some flunkey has to go and fetch them.)

I noticed that some of the bookies were eyeing the Queen's handbag with trepidation. It was the biggest handbag I have ever seen, made of the skin of a sabre-toothed tiger with the enormous teeth cleverly used to form the fastening catch. Apart from accommodating her woad, bone comb, back-scratcher, stone crown and other necessities, it was hard to understand why it was so big. Later, however, I was to learn that if she ever spotted anything she liked when visiting anybody's cave, especially antiques which she collected, she would simply pop it into her handbag. If the object was too big for the bag she would simply point a fat finger at it and announce: 'I should be graciously pleased to accept that. I'll send round for it in the morning.' It was the handbag's other function which was exercising the bookies' attention, however. She regularly hit people with it, and sometimes they never rose again in one piece. Being handbagged by the Queen was a punishment to remember, one which would become a tradition with later female leaders, and perhaps even with some males the way things are going.

The Queen gave the money-sacks to her bodyguard to count and while they did that, coin by coin – the bodyguard was clearly no mathematician and kept losing count – we all remained silent, though I could hear some intrusive noise which came from the losing dogs who were drowning their sorrows in the wattle and daub beer bower.

When finally satisfied with her winnings, the Queen deigned to speak to me.

'Well done Dido! With a name so like mine I realised you just had to be a winner. So I put the lot on your nose, which I also noticed was suitably long. The rest of the punters must have been stupid not to see that – which was just as well because that would have lowered the odds. But then they are stupid, thank Dog.'

I nodded agreement, though it had not occurred to me that she would be so silly as to back me just on the coincidence of our names, but I have since gathered that this remains common practice.

'Here is your splendid trophy,' she said, handing me the Amesbury Cup. It had been fashioned from the upper part of the skull of some hapless creature, silver not then being available. It might well have been human, perhaps belonging to someone who had offended the Queen on one of her moody days and been handbagged, but in that case it would have had to have been someone with a very big head. It was an ugly piece and I thought at the time that I would have to be very hard up for a bone to gnaw it.

'You will let me know when you are running again won't you?' the Queen said, rather menacingly.

'Like hell I will,' I thought, while smiling graciously. I might lose and there was no way that I wanted to end up as garters round those knobbly knees, especially now that I had seen them at close quarters. No wonder there was no King! In any case, I am not one to push my luck and the chance of emerging unscathed from the slalom again was zero.

Realising that the Queen had no intention of handing me the prize money, which I had seen artfully deposited in her handbag, I bowed and walked away with my trophy but had not gone far when I was accosted by the also-rans, minus Caradog and Jock Strapp who were undergoing treatment. They had obviously been drinking heavily in the beer bower to drown their sorrows, the modern word 'stoned' not being unconnected with the ancient stadium.

'Who is this bloody Dido?' one of them shouted. 'Is she registered under Wiltshire Punt Rules?'

'Where do you come from?' another one asked, aggressively.

'Berkshire,' I said proudly, but, as it turned out, rashly.

'Berkshire?' they chorused so loudly that the Queen heard them.

She went chocolate in the face as she shouted, 'We are at war with Berkshire! We hate Berkshire and everybody in it!' It was a racist remark and politically incorrect but the race relations industry had not been invented either. Clearly, though, I was an even bigger outsider than I had realised.

'Seize that dog!' Didoicea commanded. 'She is probably a spy!'

They moved towards me with their fangs bared so I threw the Amesbury Cup at them and while they were squabbling over it I scarpered back into consciousness.

Now I never see a sports stadium on television without thinking of Stonehenge and the part played by dogs in its incredible history. I am sure that my discovery will do a great deal for British Heritage. Far more people are likely to visit the world's first race-track than just another old temple.

CHAPTER 11
Van Dog

It was the hottest day of the year and as I nodded off in the shade of my favourite cherry tree I was surprised, at first, to find myself sitting alone at a table in a French bistro with a cup of coffee and an absinthe and the patron eyeing me with a suspicious look. He seemed to know that I hadn't a sou in the world, if only because I had no place to keep one, and, pending the arrival of a cheque from my brother – sent, I regret to say, as a means of keeping me away from home – the only way I could pay would be by offering yet another of my paintings which he thought were ghastly, a view with which I did not entirely dissent, being excessively self-critical. Nevertheless I had tried to assure him many times that, one day, he or his descendants would wish he had bought them all. I even told him that he would eventually advertise his wretched little café with the placard 'Dido van Dog drank here', but his only response had been to raise his eyes to the heavens and shrug.

Outside it was even hotter than it had been in the real world, a few minutes ago, for this was Arles, in Provence, and how and why – especially why – I was there were questions which the day-dreaming brain never answers. However, having heard the Chap bang on for so long about modern art, it was not all that surprising that I should imagine myself as a painter, by which I mean a dauber on canvas rather than on doors and window-frames. In real life I had fancied myself, for some time, as something of an avant garde sculptor. It seems that all one has to do to be a successful sculptor in stone is to bore interesting holes in it, so why shouldn't this also apply to bones? Certainly, the moment that I have completed a lick-out of a sizeable marrowbone it becomes more interesting in aesthetic terms, comparable, in my view, with the works of professional hole-makers like Dame Barbecue Yapworth and Ilkley Moore. Why shouldn't craftsdogship with my tongue be just as meritorious as crafts-manship with human hands? Indeed, I could reasonably argue that it is not only more difficult but more artistic, being entirely natural, while human sculptors have to use artificial tools, like hammers and chisels. Of course, I have gone much further than just licking out holes. With my teeth I have created some very weird shapes in bone which critics might well describe as 'full of dynamic vitality', 'subtle' or even 'witty'.

When creating them I did, at least, work on my medium to change its shape in an imaginative manner while some so-called sculptors, these days, simply lump together existing objects like building bricks, bits of scrap metal, old tyres, dead sheep and – quite appallingly – stuffed puppy-dogs, without doing any work on them at all. They claim that it is the relationship between the bits that makes them art, when what they mean is 'artful' because some galleries and individuals are stupid enough to buy these pathetic efforts, while city councils egg the 'sculptors' on by giving them grants from public money to do even worse. It would seem obvious to the meanest canine mentality that, to qualify as art, an object must be the product of superior skill, as it was with such sculptors as Dogatello and still is with some, like my friend, the justly famous animal sculptor Jonathan Kennelworthy.

I reckon that, by modern standards, I have made a few mistresspieces by gnawing large bones into subtle shapes exhibiting such a poignant rhythm that they ought to have been bought for the nation. Sadly, however, I could not resist chewing on and thereby destroying the *objets d'art*. A heap of my finer tooth-chiselled bones, suitably arranged to stress the artistic rapport between them, should surely be worthy of permanent exhibition and, perhaps I have been remiss in not giving sufficient thought to posterity. The trouble is that, to a canine connoisseur, a bone in the mouth is worth ten in the Tate.

They say that art lies in concealing art and I can claim to be exceptionally adept at that. I have buried many of my works so cleverly that the Chap has not even been aware of their existence until he chanced to find them months or even years later while digging in some border, patio tub or window-box. No doubt they were then of even greater aesthetic value, having acquired a patina which only time can endow, as happens with buried bronzes.

Anyway, it was not as a sculptor but as a painter that I was sitting in the café which, I recall, had become known through my regular patronage as Le Chien Qui Fume, which, in fact, I didn't because only humans are mad enough to ruin their health by smoking. What had happened was that, for dramatic effect, I sometimes sat with a large pipe in my mouth but never lit it.

Being entirely self-taught, as I was in sculpture, I had been driven to invent my own method of painting. One obvious way would have been to use my tail as a brush but I knew that this had been done by a donkey, whose works were hailed by critics who had been led to believe that they were created by human hands. An ape, called Congo, had achieved similar success with his hands. So instead, as it had served me so well in my sculpture, I decided to make my mouth my main tool for painting in oils. All I did was to pick up each tube of paint, as the artistic mood took me, unscrew the cap and simply squirt it with my jaws on to the canvas without using a brush. The results were sensational to say the least. Until then paintings had been flat. In mine the paint stuck out in such wavy lumps that it was truly three-dimensional and I found I could vary the results by lying the canvas flat on the ground and squirting the paint from various heights.

There were times, if I was in the mood, when I spread the paint around a bit with my paws or even my nose, which looked odd as a result if I forgot to wipe it, as I usually did. Once, after I turned round sharply and brushed my tail on the wet canvas by accident, I realised that it lent panache to the overall effect. So I occasionally employed that technique too, using vigorous strokes, and it was all enormous fun. Usually, though, I just let the tube do the job, the art being in the way it was held and waggled. Of course this meant that I went through a hell of lot of tubes, which ran me into serious debt with the paint shop, but there had been plenty of precedents for that: Rembrandt, for instance, in his hard-up days.

Ever searching for my concept of beauty, I sometimes chose the colour of the natural object on which I was concentrating as I did, for example, when I was painting my bright yellow beanbag, creating a picture which, though a bit crude, I sensed was probably fated to be famous one day. I can just see it being described by critics trying to fill their columns in the glossy magazines – 'a symbol of stability in her world of continual crisis', or 'showing her deep respect for inanimate objects' when the only reason I painted it was because it was raining that day and, being a compulsive painter, I needed a subject to pass the time and the beanbag was handy. As I recall that beanbag was rather uncomfortable, being understuffed, and not really very pretty.

I used yellow to a degree which has since caused art historians to theorise in all manner of intricate ways about my reasons for doing so. You know: 'She was besotted with the sun, the fount of all existence', 'Her mood was so black that she compensated for it with the brightest colour', and all that nonsense. The simple truth is that I liked yellow partly because it is a nice bright colour in a dull world but mainly because my supplier happened to have such a big stock of it that he offered me two tubes for the price of one to get rid of it. This was one of the reasons why I painted so many sunflowers. Another was the fact that the sunflowers I used as subjects were handy in the fields and were free, which was also the real explanation of why I did so many portraits of myself. Art experts would say later that my self-portraits 'showed that I was braced against the shock of what I saw in the mirror'. Rubbish! And what a damned cheek! I painted myself because, again like Rembrandt, I couldn't afford models. The critics also said that I 'found my inspiration among the poor', as though that was something particularly laudable, but I didn't know anybody else once I had left home. I would have been very happy to paint the rich if I had known any. My few friends, like the postman and his son, posed for me for nothing when I assured them that they stood a chance of making themselves immortal in the process. It had been a joke, of course, though there's many a true word spoken in jest, especially in the art world. Like other painters, my priority was not fame in the distant future but filling my belly each day. After all, what had posterity done for me?, as the Hollywood dogul Sam Golden-Retriever once asked so trenchantly.

At other times, such as when painting clouds for instance, I just let rip with the handiest tube. I had quite a lot of blue tubes too, which was why I often used that colour, as I did when I tried my paw at putting my idea of a starry night on canvas. The stars ended up looking more like Catherine wheels and the wisps of cloud like waves on a stormy sea, which was not what I wanted at all but had been the best I could do. The trouble was that when I'd stuck on as much paint as I did there was no way of changing it except to stick on more. The result horrified a lot of people at the time, including the bistro-keeper, but, as excess is in the eye of the beholder and fashions in art change as much as fashion in clothes, I reckon that even my worst paintings, like Starry Night, might be worth money one day. At least nobody could say that I was not 'bold with colour' but, then, who can't be, given a few tubes and the urge to have a go, especially at cut price?

My efforts were so unlike those of any other artist that art historians of the future would have no problem ascribing my works to me because I signed them all, boldly, with my first name, Dido, rather than Dido van Dog. I judged this to be sufficiently distinctive for, though I was remote from things in Arles, I was pretty confident that nobody else with that name was operating in the painting field. The great thing for a painter is to have a name that catches on, like Michelangelo or Leonardo da Vinci, and I reckoned that Dido van Dog was a good one that should endure, with copyists of my style calling themselves Didoists and their method Didoism.

Being a loner is sad for any dog which, by its nature, requires regular contact and affection, but the trouble was that in Arles at that time the few other dogs were flea-ridden curs with no more culture or taste than the flea-ridden peasants, so I kept as clear of both as I could. This gave me the reputation for being eccentric, which I suppose I was for various other reasons, apart from sucking the empty tobacco pipe. I got a lot of my best imaginative ideas while lying upside down on my back because so many things look better that way, the Chap for instance, to name but one. People thought this was barmy but, then, they hadn't tried it. I was, also, the first artist to paint there under a burning sun in a fur coat, having, of course, no option. I did not even wear a hat, as everyone else did against the sun, because I could not find one that would stay on as it is often windy there.

When I was living in Paris and frequenting the Dome café, talking nonsense about light and how much canvas to leave bare with painters like Tooloose Lowtrick (when he could tear himself away from the brothels), Nightgas (who specialised in ballet girls), Doget (who liked picnicking with naked ladies) and Sewerrat (who painted everything in dots), I had worn a floppy velvet hat – chocolate of course – but it would have looked out of place in Provence. Anyway, I did not want to be reminded of Paris which, like most capital cities, is an inhuman place where neither people nor dogs are free to move around, and there are even more frogs than in the country. In Arles I had tried to conform with the rural practice by wearing wooden sabots, but I can assure you that they are not made for dogs and I would have looked ridiculous in four of them.

I suppose I also looked funny because my easel was so small, and who had heard of a painter who hardly ever used a brush? I did not use a palette at all, and the sight of my nose all smeared with paint made me look so odd that the boys laughed and threw stones at me, no doubt egged on by their parents. I tended to paint very fast, squirting the tubes with my mouth in quick succession because I did not want the paint to dry too quickly in the hot sun, and this led to stories that I was painting in a frenzy. My pictures of cypresses looked like flames and people said it was because my brain was on fire. In fact it was the best I could do with my tubes, not deliberate at all. Since then, of course, mouth-painting, which I pioneered, has become common among disabled people and is not regarded as odd.

All things considered, though, I suppose it was not surprising that my eccentricity was soon converted to madness in the locals' minds, with murmurs that I should be put away for my own safety as well as theirs. Actually, I was no madder than anyone else in that dog-forsaken place, just different and less inhibited. I was constantly afraid that they were coming to lock me up, as the world mistreats so many of its geniuses, but I was not going to change my behaviour for anyone. Artists are supposed to have licence to be odd and whatever I was I was determined to be the only one of it because I find uniformity and conformity so boring! Sadly, it is the fate of all innovators, whether human or canine, to be regarded as mad, especially if they happen to be loners, as they often are.

I had not been a loner all the time in Arles. I had been foolish enough to invite another painter whom I had met in Paris, called Paul Goget, to stay with me with the idea of forming a co-operative colony of artists. He turned out to be a nasty piece of work, as I should have known because he spoke out of the side of his mouth which is a sure sign of untrustworthiness in a dog and, I suspect, in a man. I found I could not relax in his company because he gave me the uneasy feeling that whenever there was not much in the larder, which was most of the time because he was more broke than I was, he might be planning to have my liver for breakfast. He could never see anybody else's side of an argument. For example, I spent a long time trying to convince him that a dog, like myself, is a work of art while a man or a woman is not, in spite of all the paintings made of the human body. What any man or woman looks like is purely fortuitous, the results of millions of years of natural evolution over which humans have had no control. Any dog, however, is a deliberate work of art created by human breeders through conscious selection from our original wolf like form over many generations. Though the breeders have produced a few indifferent or even ugly works of art, they have done a superbly beautiful job on some of us and especially on the Labrador. Even those dogs that look as though they were put together by Picasso can still be regarded as art. Goget was so besotted with the human body, especially the female which he couldn't paint anyway, that he lost his temper with both me and my argument.

I didn't like his style of painting either. Like me, he was bold with colour but he was what I call a flat painter with no sense of perspective and the females on whom he concentrated were ugly, with their limbs out of proportion. He tried to argue that there can be no such thing as ugly art but it depends who is looking at it. If beauty is in the eye of the beholder then so is ugliness. As for that other universally held misapprehension that beauty is truth, ugliness is equally true, as so many human beings appreciate when they look in the mirror first thing in the morning – something which dogs rarely experience, except in extreme old age.

As I have said, art lies in concealing art but some artists conceal it so well that there is none of it to be seen. I agree that the creative power of the artist lies in selecting some things for emphasis and omitting others, but there cannot be any art when everything is omitted. Yet some modern daubers present canvases that are totally black or totally white, canvases with a few straight lines on them or even completely blank canvases with a couple of buttons sewn on, and claim them all as art. I suppose the argument is that all the rest that should be there was in the mind of the artist but he could not be bothered to put it down.

Nevertheless he still feels that, as he has 'stated his message', society should support him in his great endeavours.

Sometimes, people calling themselves artists just cut things out of magazines and stick them on their canvases, dignifying the puppish result by calling it découpage or décollage. All you need in the world of so-called abstract art, apart from a pair of scissors, is brass nerve and perhaps a higher degree of self-delusion than most people. I call these people con-artists because what they are good at is abstracting money from the public. There are usually some people who convince themselves that there must be something in it and others, usually dealers, who believe they can build up a cult about some artist and make a lot of money out of him as well as for him. It is quite amazing what humans can be induced to believe about art by arguments or blind belief that would never fool a dog.

Of course, Goget lost his temper again when beaten in this argument, especially when I told him that I had more draughtsdogship in my nose than he had draughtsmanship in the whole of his body. He started to fling my few things around so violently that I nipped him in the calf to calm him down. That was how the rumour started that I tried to murder him. How these simple events become exaggerated with time in the human mind, which does not happen in the mental dog world!

Friendship can be a rough old game and I was very relieved when Goget took off in a huff to Tahiti, where he died, leaving scores of paintings that have since sold for millions. I wonder what will happen to mine. My painting of irises, for instance. Frankly, I did not think it was very good, and certainly far from being my best, but human stupidity knows no limits and some idiot might pay millions for it one day. After all one American artist called, I believe, Bandy Warhorse or something like that made a fortune out of painting cans of dogmeat, or was it soup? Meanwhile, I would endure the Frogs and their dull backwater for a few more months and, if my pictures continued to fail to sell, I would write a boring bestseller about a year in Provence.

As I was thinking along these lines in that café in Arles, while the sun blazed down relentlessly outside, and hoping that the patron would accept my painting of my yellow beanbag as payment for my coffee and absinthe, three rough-looking customers, whom I had seen around, sat themselves down at the next table. They already seemed full of wine and it was not long before I realised that I was the butt of their jokes, to which I was well used.

'Why is that bitch sporting a *tricolore* on her conk?' the one with the biggest wine-belly asked, referring to my paint-stained nose. 'I hear she's not even French.'

'She say's she's a Labrador, but who ever saw a brown one?' the little one said. 'I think she's a boxer.'

'I think you're right,' said the fat man. 'But shouldn't a boxer have cropped ears?' he asked, referring to the revolting French habit of cutting a boxer's ears to make them smaller and more pointed, a mutilation which is prohibited in more civilised countries.

'Yes, you're right!' the third one said, producing a clasp knife and opening it ominously. 'Let's crop them now.'

They grabbed me before I realised that they meant to do it. I felt a terrible pain in the flap of my right ear and woke up to find I had been pressing it on the sharp edge of the bone which I had been sculpting before I had dozed off. A few drops of blood had trickled down the bone making an unusual pattern. Had I been Picasso and described myself as 'a dog in revolt against her destiny', I could have let the blood dry, given the piece a dramatic name like 'The Tears of War', and put it on the market for a million dollars confident that some idiot, whom I privately despised, would buy it.

P.S. (*Post Somnium*)

I never sold a single picture in my lifetime, but long after my death the one of my little yellow beanbag sold for ten million pounds while my irises were bought by some Japanese for more than twenty million! There was a phase when prints of my cypresses, my chrysanthemums and the postman's son were on every suburban wall. The way you humans fail to appreciate artists until they are dead and cannot reap the benefit of their works is ridiculous. Why should being dead make such a difference? I have a feeling that it wouldn't matter now what I had painted or how I had painted it. People would still pay millions for it, especially if I had signed it. I produced some awful pictures, real daubs like Starry Night, but you try convincing the owners of that! Or the dealers who flogged them!

CHAPTER 12

Too Close for Comfort

It has been said – rather often of late, I fear – that fame has made me vain. If by that people mean that it has made me more aware of my potential I might agree, but dogs are never vain in the human sense, though some of us may seem to be, especially those who appear in the showring. No! Vanity, meaning conceit of one's personal qualities or attainments, is essentially a human attribute and rarely was that made more obvious to me than one very hot afternoon when the Chap and I were trout fishing on the Kennet, at Littlecote near Hungerford, right on the Berkshire–Wiltshire border.

As there was nothing much moving and the river looked dead the Chap would soon have taken me home and I would have been happy to go because it was not long to my feeding time, but my friend Peter, the river-keeper, walked up the bank to see us. I thought he just wanted a chat but he had a message.

'There's a man who has come down from London to interview you,' he said to the Chap. 'Could you spare him a few minutes? I didn't know how long it would take me to find you so I sent him up to the big house to have a look round while he waits.'

'Who is he?' the Chap asked, not being willing to be interviewed by any Tom or Dick, though Harrys were usually all right.

'I didn't get his name but I think he's from the BBC,' Peter replied. 'He has quite a big camera crew so it's obviously important. He must have tried to get you at home and found nobody there.'

'Oh, I suppose some spy has died suddenly and they want me to talk about him,' the Chap said, loftily, being used to such requirements. 'I'll walk up to the big house and I'd better take Dido with me. It's far too hot to leave her in the car. She's allowed in the house on a lead. She's been in before.'

We looked into the Great Hall of the splendid Tudor mansion, with its unique collection of Cromwellian arms and armour festooning the walls. There was no sign of a camera crew and the only man there pointed up towards the Haunted Landing. I knew that spot well. It was by the bedroom where Wild Will Darrell, a former owner of the place in the seventeenth century, had burned his newly born illegitimate baby on the fire and the midwife had, bravely, grassed on him.

As we climbed the stairs I noticed a camera team, mostly in jeans and T-shirts, in the corner of the landing taking pictures of us as we approached and a nattily dressed man, who was vaguely familiar. As the man turned round he was clearly trying to hide something large behind his back and the Chap recognised him right away, with a gasp of 'Oh God!' It was Michael Aspirin, the presenter of the TV programme *This Is Your Life!*

The Chap looked thoroughly annoyed for he has always said that if he was ever put in that position by some trick or other he would just flounce out because, I suspect, there is so much in his personal past he needs to hide that he would be scared stiff about who might suddenly be produced on the programme. However, as such publicity never comes amiss to any author, especially in these days when books sell on hype and not on merit, and because his vanity was tickled, I think he was having second thoughts about what to do when he really had reason to be annoyed. Moving towards us, producing his big red book with a flourish and totally ignoring the Chap, Aspirin bent down and announced, in my ear, 'Dido, this is your life!' I was thrilled for I would never spurn a boost to my fame and I had nothing to fear from anyone in my past life. Or so I thought.

Before either of us could recover our poise we were bustled into the Long Gallery, a huge room where there were more cameras, a big TV screen and a few faces I recognised, including several dogs. I spotted the Boss, who must have been in on the plot to ambush us and had not told the Chap, fearing that he might veto it. I was also pleased to see my paperback publishers, Francesca and Jenny, and Angela Rippon, who had interviewed me when I was in the Parade of Dog Personalities at Crufts.

Among the dogs, I was especially thrilled to see the handsome figure of Bugler, the chocolate father of my seven chocolate pups. I felt I could trust him not to go into too much detail about our rather unusual, on-and-off, three-day affair when I had given him such a runaround. It would not be good for my literary image to be made to sound like a female version of Alan Clark though, on the other paw, it does sell books. Seeing Bugler, and the look he gave me, made me feel broody again but, while I hope that I am not a snob, I was not at all pleased to see Charlie, the village Jack Russell who haunts me, in the line-up. That little sod gets in everywhere and, as he seems to spend his life fantasising about me, I was concerned about what false boasts he might make or hint at, if given the microphone. You know what some chaps are like, especially little ones.

The television ordeal held no sweat for me. As a result of so many appearances in connection with my books, I am now an old hand at dealing with TV interviewers – even those crazy ones on *The Big Breakfast* – and if you can cope with them with aplomb, as I certainly did when I appeared on their programme, well . . . So, at Mr Aspirin's invitation, I settled back in a comfortable chair for what I foresaw as a pleasant trip down Memory Lane.

Wasting no time, Aspirin began: 'You were born in Devon, the seventh pup of a litter of seven so, obviously, Fate intended you to be something special. Here is someone you should recognise from your puppy days though, as happens with most dogs through no fault of their own, you have never seen her since.'

The face of an older chocolate Labrador, but looking very like me, appeared on the big screen.

'Hello, Dido! This is your mother, Tarka. Your father and I are sorry that we cannot be with you on this great day but we are not as young as we were. We have followed your career with great pride and particularly admire the way you have organised it and your general life so that your Chap does all the work for you while you get all the credit. That is how things should be in the dog–man relationship and I am sure you will keep it that way. Well done daughter! Keep working for the rights of dogdom!'

Tears came to my eyes as the picture faded. Mother had done all seven of us so proud. I have a picture of us all looking as fat as butter. It was sad that we didn't meet, but Devon is a long way. As I wiped my eyes with my paw Aspirin was off on another spiel.

'You were named, at the Kennel Club, as Keneven Fantasy but that was changed for everyday use to Dido by someone who bought you when you were only eight weeks old and took you to live on a farm in Berkshire.'

Another face appeared on the screen and I recognised it as Alison, my first mistress, who was speaking by satellite all the way from Australia. I am doubly grateful to her because, when she had decided to emigrate to the other side of the world and could not take me with her, she had found the Chap and the Boss just when they were in their most receptive mood, being dogless after losing their last springer spaniel. As I was the first Labrador they have ever had in their pack they have been especially grateful ever since. It was Alison who changed my name to Dido, after the great queen who founded the ancient city of Carthage, when she spotted it in her mother's classical dictionary. Though it may be a funny name it is a good one because everyone remembers it.

'Hello Dido!' Alison said. 'Congratulations on your great success as a writer and canine personality. Do you remember when you were kicked by that horse?'

Did I remember! How could I ever forget it. It was absolute hell. My leg was so badly injured that I had to undergo several operations and I took such a dislike to the vet who did them that he had to muzzle me, young as I was. Ever since, I shudder and shiver every time I see any vet or smell one. Lots of women are the same about mice, though with the Boss it is snakes, even the sight of one on television, that kind of fear being something that cuts right across intellect, human or canine.

Suddenly, we could hear so much noise outside in the grounds that the recording had to be interrupted while the windows were all closed, stifling as it was. When the programme was restarted I was delighted to hear the amiable Scottish tones of Bill Meldrum, the head keeper from Sandringham who is also the Queen's chief dog man. He it was who was kind enough to draw Her Majesty's attention to my first book, following which I received a treasured note from Buckingham Palace.

It all seemed to be going swimmingly when I heard another voice from the past which I thought I recognised.

'Hello Dido! I'm glad to see you looking in the pink, or should I say in the chocolate . . .'

I began to shake. Could it be him? It was – that bloody vet and in the flesh! In he walked, white coat and all, smelling clinical, like vets do. I know that it was illogical and that he had done his best for me, for which I should be grateful because not a sign of that injury remains, but that is not how panic works is it? Unprofessional as it undoubtedly was, I just flipped and I was out of the Long Gallery like a scalded dog. On the way I ripped out several television cables in a shower of sparks and was down the stairs, through the Great Hall and into the grounds, which had long been a theme park.

It was only then that I realised what all the outside noise had been. I ran straight into a seventeenth-century mock battle between Cavaliers and Roundheads staged by an outfit called The Sealed Knot. Grown men, armed with swords, pikes and other weapons of the period and who clearly enjoyed fantasising by dressing up in period costumes, were struggling in a rather half-hearted way with arguments, here and there, about who should pretend to be dead. It was the men who won the verbal arguments that laid down on the grass, being glad of the opportunity for a rest in that heat and with all those clothes on. I could see that they were all taking it seriously and I wondered what their wives thought about them. We play a few games in the dog world in which we only pretend to fight and even pretend to submit, but I don't think we could ever go to such lengths without feeling silly. There could be no doubt what the chief attraction was – dressing up which, these days, is supposed to be essentially a female vanity, though it was not so in the past.

Fearing that Aspirin and his lot would be after me to induce me to resume the programme, vet and all, and realising that there was no personal danger whatever in the conflict, I saw the mass of struggling humanity, who were re-fighting the Battle of Newbury, as a perfect place in which to lose myself. I had to choose a side and, as I was short-haired, I had to be a Roundhead though all my sympathies were with the Cavaliers. In my heart I couldn't really support that self-righteous bastard Cromwell, the so-called 'Protector' who destroyed half of Britain's history. We have been to so many castles, from Donington to Pontefract, which were destroyed by that Bible-punching villain, who was vain enough to believe that he was guided by God. He and his boring Puritans even prohibited horseracing, another thing for which Newbury has it in for him, and I have a strong feeling that he did not like dogs.

However, I happened to know that the Roundheads had won the Battle of Newbury and the Chap has always said that it pays to be on the winning side so I pitched in and bit the leg of the first Cavalier I encountered, though not very hard. I had thought of nipping back to the Great Hall to look for some small-size armour – the men all seem to have been small in those days – but the thought of meeting up with the vet stopped me in my tracks. I would fight on naked, except for my collar. Once in the mêlée I found that so many of the Cavaliers smelt of strong drink that I could see why their side lost.

Aspirin and his crew, accompanied by the vet, appeared at the edge of the battle ground and, at the prospect of appearing on TV themselves, the contestants upped their effort, which had become very laboured and painfully concerned with preventing any injury, several of the slain arising from the dead so that they could be seen by the cameras taking a more active role. Spotting me in the middle, Aspirin began offering substantial bribes to anyone who would catch me and, as these increased in value, the whole Sealed Knot, Cavaliers and Roundheads alike, set aside their historic differences and were after me. They hadn't a man's chance as I knew the Littlecote grounds like the back of my paw. I was soon away from the mob, weighed down as they were in their armour, and was making for the main entrance when I saw that my path was blocked by a contingent of fully armed and helmeted Roman soldiers who were making for the theme park where they too were to stage a mock battle involving several engines of war including a giant wheeled catapult, which they were pulling. Littlecote was once a Roman encampment and while some men fantasise by dressing up in seventeenth-century garb others make an enormous effort to go back a couple of thousand years or so, limiting their weapons to spears, swords and shields. Apart from their plumed helmets, their costumes were certainly better suited to the hot weather.

As they take great pains to be as lifelike as possible in every respect some of the latter-day Romans started shouting in Latin, beginning with

'Cave canem', which made sense, but then throwing in anything they could summon up from their schooldays, like 'Quo vadis?', 'Quod erat demonstrandum' and 'In flagrante delicto'. I don't know whether the leader fancied himself as Julius Caesar but I heard him shout, 'Et tu, Brute,' which I did not take as a compliment. I was about to reply 'Beware the Ides of March, cleverdick,' but I didn't know the Latin for 'cleverdick', even in dog-Latin, and I could see a few of the Roundheads still in pursuit, all the Cavaliers having quit the chase for the beer tent. Being genetically allergic to being harried on two fronts, I sped through the gateway leading to the theme park shopping centre. What confronted me there was even worse: a troop of armoured knights on gaily caparisoned horses, the jousting team on its way to the theme park tilt-yard. Oh my Dog! I thought. Not another encounter with a horse with that vet on hand!

There was only one escape route: into the Fairy Grotto, a narrow place for children where nobody on horseback could pursue me. I passed the giant toadstools and the little gnomes' house then found I could just squeeze in through the tiny door of the Fairy Queen's palace. Nobody else could get in and nobody would think of looking for me there.

I had barely recovered my breath when Aspirin and some of his crew walked slowly past my hiding place, having given up the unequal struggle.

'I was always warned never to do any programme with animals,' Aspirin said dispiritedly, looking as though he needed one, or even two, of his namesake tablets to combat the headache I had given him. 'I'll certainly never do it again. Damn that dog! Making me look a fool like that! All that time and effort wasted! All those people brought here for nothing and their expenses still to be paid. We'll just have to cut our losses and get the hell out of here.'

On their way back to the big house to collect their equipment they spotted my friend Eddy, the blacksmith at the theme park, who always knows everything concerning local matters – his smithy is a great gossip shop – and was well appraised of what had been happening. I rather suspect that he had seen me slip into the Fairy Grotto, which is next to his smithy, but anyway, bless him, when Aspirin asked him if he had seen a fugitive chocolate Labrador he said 'Yes, she went thataway,' pointing his hammer towards the river. 'It's strictly private down there,' Eddy added in his fruity, Wiltshire accent.

The Chap and I have a long-standing arrangement that if ever we get parted on the river, because I have wandered off, we would meet up at Eddy's, where it is always warm on a chilly day. So I knew he would eventually look for me there and as soon as the coast was clear I joined Eddy and hid behind his big anvil in case anyone reappeared. Nobody did and we soon heard the van which had brought the camera crew roar away off the premises, to be followed by the cars which had ferried down the witnesses to my life, including the vet who had caused all the trouble.

'Good riddance!' I said aloud.

Sure enough, after a few minutes the Chap joined me there, his relief at finding that I was OK temporarily overcoming his annoyance, because he had been blamed for my behaviour. I agreed that, in view of book sales these days, it was a pity to have missed the publicity, but the Chap's Chinese mind had already decided how to turn that to our advantage.

'As soon as we get home I'll give the story of how you outwitted *This Is Your Life* to the newspapers. They love knocking the BBC, especially if they can cut one of their personalities down to size in the process. I can just see the headline: "BBC Fiasco As Dog Snubs Star Presenter!"'

In view of the previous hour or so I was thinking that, in my case, the programme might have been better called *This Was Your Strife* when I stirred and found myself on the riverbank. The heat had sent me into a doze, with the Chap, who was still snoring gently, stretched out alongside me.

CHAPTER 13
Paradise Lost

As the Arabs allow only the saluki, their favourite hunting dog, to enter their tents and houses, regarding all other breeds as unclean, I never thought that I would be grateful to their culture. However, it looks as though I have to thank them for the greatest imaginable reason – my best hope of eventually enjoying eternal life in paradise, along with my Chap and the Boss if they chance to get there in their due course.

Alone of all the great religions, Islam offers dogs a sure place there – all dogs, not just salukis. I know that because of the results of my unique, real-life researches into the question of canine immortality which will come as a shock to many of my readers and to their pets. Let me explain this situation, which is dog's honest truth and nothing to do with any of my bone-dreams.

In view of all the wonderful services which dogs perform for the human species – companionship, guiding the blind, helping the deaf to hear, comforting the sick and combating crime – I had always assumed that the best of us should be eligible for entry to paradise when our time comes. However, because of something the present Pope was misquoted as saying in that connection, the Chap had reason to make some top-level inquiries on my behalf. As he had a nodding acquaintance with Cardinal Basil Hume, the head of the Roman Catholic Church in Britain, we decided to consult him first. I thought the approach looked promising because, before he became the Archbishop of Westminster, the Cardinal had been Professor of Dogmatic Theology. The issue was far from being just academic because so many people really do expect to meet up with their pets in the next world.

The Chap asked the Cardinal for the Church's latest view on the question of whether or not animals, and dogs in particular, possess immortal souls which are capable of ending up in paradise, as humans are supposed to. His Eminence's brief but courteous reply showed that he clearly did not wish to involve himself in this theological problem, and he referred us to the Catholic Study Circle for Animal Welfare, whose many supporters argue that it is inconceivable that any of God's creatures should be banned from paradise. In our dealings with the Study Circle we learned that Cardinal Hume had upset them by insisting that it was impossible for animals of any kind, even chocolate Labradors like me, to possess an immortal soul so we could never get even as far as scratching on the pearly gates.

We therefore decided to go right to the top and consult the Vatican itself, and after a few weeks' delay in which documents and authorities were consulted, we received a kind reply from the Assessor at the Vatican, one Monsignor Sepe, written on beautiful paper watermarked with the Pope's insignia, the triple tiara and the crossed keys of St Peter. Monsignor Sepe assured us that it had always been the teaching of the Roman Church that animals *do* possess souls because God breathes life into them. This sounded great, but then came the bad news: they are not immortal souls. This suggestion that there are first- and second-class souls was new to us and to many others to whom we have passed on this pronouncement. What is the purpose of a soul, I ask, if it is not immortal? Does it die like the body? I always thought that the whole point about a soul was that it was not destroyed at death.

The trouble is that, though the Christian religion began as an attempt to modify and improve the older Jewish faith, it has always remained stuck with Genesis, the first book of the Old Testament, which insists that only Man, meaning *Homo sapiens* and including women of course, was made in the image of God and is therefore unique in possessing an immortal soul. It follows, therefore, that only human beings can qualify for paradise because, since all other creatures lack an immortal soul, there is nothing of them to go there or anywhere else. All those animals so intimately associated with the Christian story – the lambs, sheep, asses, oxen, even the dove of peace – are barred, along with all the rest of non-human creation including dogs and cats.

To my mind the Vatican seemed to be splitting whiskers so we decided to consult the Archbishop of Canterbury as to the official attitude of the Anglican Church in the hope that it might be more enlightened. The reply, on his behalf, stated that since the Church of England has never made any official pronouncement on the subject there are 'different strands of theological opinion' about it and, by coincidence, one of them was shortly to be made public. At a meeting of the British Association for the Advancement of Science, Dr John Habgood, then Archbishop of York, indicated that he believed apes have such a measure of consciousness that they may have souls and end up in heaven when they die. Surely, I thought, if he is prepared to extend immortality to apes he can hardly exclude monkeys or any other intelligent creatures, like dogs. And when his colleague the Archdeacon of York, the Venerable George Austin, commented that most people would be very disappointed to get to heaven and find that their pets were not there, the Chap immediately contacted the Archbishop. He kindly replied including his learned scientific paper, with the comment that it might be hard going for me which, frankly, it was.

By the same post, from another source, we received a much older view propounded by John Wesley, the founder of Methodism, who argued, rightly in my opinion, that as a recompense for what many animals suffer on earth they will enjoy 'happiness without end' because the justice of God demands it. Sadly, however, the more we thought about it the more obvious it became that, fundamentally, all the Christian Churches are still saddled with the pronouncements of Genesis, especially in England where the Reformation of the Church under Henry the Eighth, a staunch Catholic, was only marginal.

Of course if any religion is stuck with Genesis it should be the Jewish faith, but we thought it wise to seek the official guidance of the former Chief Rabbi, Lord Jakobovits. Let the dog see the rabbi, I have always urged, but in the end we could only write to him. Sure enough, he told us that while Judaism accepts some form of salvation for man and animal alike it 'does not hold that animals are created in the Divine Image, nor do they enjoy immortality or resurrection'. So not even kosher creatures make it to paradise.

Apparently, the theologians raise two further objections to us as candidates for heaven: we are not 'rational' and have no free will, which are features unique to Man, but I would dispute that. Everything I do has a sensible purpose and I behave less stupidly than many humans, who are repeatedly referred to as sheep in some religions. Furthermore, though my free will is restricted by human requirements, I make plenty of choices the way I want to. Just ask the Chap!

I suspect that it is an intriguing complication of Judgement Day that fuels the theologians' determination to keep us out. Since we animals are regarded as having no concept of sin we could not be accused of committing it so, on Judgement Day, we would all have to be judged innocent with no hell for us. On the other hand, according to Holy Writ, only a proportion of the human souls will be deemed fit for entry to paradise. How the assembled dogs, donkeys and the rest would bark and bray their approval as those who have been cruel to us were consigned elsewhere to get their comedownance!

Both the Chap and I were cast down by the situation. If there are no dogs in paradise he doesn't want to go there, even in the unlikely circumstance of being given the option. I find it hard to believe that there is a separate paradise for animals and, if there is, I do not want to go there because without human companionship any life, and especially eternal life, would be my idea of hell.

Then, one of the many fan-letters I receive told us that the Moslem faith offers the best promise of paradise for some animals, though by no means all. Mohammed accepted the great biblical prophets, including Jesus, as very important religious figures so he decreed that those animals which had been of assistance to any of them qualify for entry to heaven. These include asses, lambs, oxen, camels, whales – for helping Jonah – doves and, happily, dogs. We were told that according to the Koran, the Moslems' holy book, a dog gave assistance to the Seven Sleepers, but we could find nobody who knew who they were. Then, by chance, the Chap dined with a Saudi Arabian shooting friend of mine, General Hashim Hashim, who has bought many of my books, signed with my pawprint, for his friends. He spent his boyhood in Mecca and claims direct descent from Mohammed so, surely, he would know who the Seven Sleepers were. He did and produced the Koran, open at the relevant page. They were seven men who went to sleep in a cave for many years, Rip van Winkle fashion, and had a dog with them who shared their slumbers and kept guard, presumably being a light sleeper.

Grateful as I am to the Prophet, I would rather not embrace Islam if I can avoid it, preferring my own culture and being anxious to avoid being a target for a fatwah, even with the glamour of a round-the-clock bodyguard at public expense. With my cavalier attitude to authority I would be sure to say or write something that would upset some ayatollah. Furthermore, Islam is alien to my nature because it means 'submission' and, while I am co-operative, I am not a submitting dog. I am an action dog and am determined to find another way into paradise – by persuading the Christian theologians to see dog-sense. Fortunately, a few like Archbishop Habgood are prepared to take a modern stand and a more sensitive view, and look forward to meeting him in paradise, if not before. Meanwhile, though, I will concentrate my assault on the Vatican which will, undoubtedly, be the hardest nut to crack. How? Read my next adventure!

CHAPTER 14

Her Eminence

The gross inequity of the Christian dog dogma continued to bug me because I felt sure that I could make some impact on the top authorities if only I could get to them and argue the issue. After all, their belief is only based on something that an old man called Moses was supposed to have written down thousands of years ago, and he might have got it wrong or been misquoted, as still happens all the time according to various politicians. I was not just thinking about myself and the rest of dogdom but about all the dear old people who bank on meeting, up with their beloved pets in paradise, not just for old acquaintances sake but because they are convinced that it would be a dull place without them. You see, the Churches believe that, with the deserving, not only will the immortal soul be resurrected in paradise but the body as well. So it should be like previous life to some extent, only better – but not if there are no dogs around!

The authorities I needed to get at first were the Pope and the Cardinals, not only because they would be the toughest nuts but because if they could be made to change their minds the others might follow. Sadly, there seemed to be no way I could ever get to them in person because they would be too busy bothering about those with first-class souls to concern themselves with our second-class jobs, and any visit to Rome meant that I would be heavily penalised by the quarantine restrictions. So, I suppose it was chronic frustration over my impotence to exert any impact on those who could do something about the problem that drove me to rack my imagination so vividly about it that, suddenly, there I was sitting in the Sistine Chapel, the ancient heart of the Vatican.

This was the place where the Conclave of Cardinals is held to elect the new Pope. There, on the left of the altar, was the papal throne with the

Pope sitting on it. There were the Cardinals, all one hundred and thirty-nine of them, in their stalls. And above us all was the recently restored ceiling by Michelangelo who, no doubt, at that moment was disporting himself in paradise in spite of his fearful fall-outs with the Pope of his day, though I wonder if it is really anything like he portrayed it. The whole scene was awfully depressing.

What was I doing there? To my astonishment, I was being installed as a Cardinal myself having been chosen by the Pope to be one of his counsellors! Fortunately, one does not have to be in Holy Orders to become a Cardinal which is why some of those old Popes were able to appoint their nephews and pals so easily. Nevertheless, I doubt that a woman can become one but there is nothing specifically in the rules to bar a bitch. As a Cardinal, these days, I would have to be celibate but then I am now anyway because the Chap and the Boss won't let me have any more pups, saying that I have done my duty in that direction. So there I was, the first canine Cardinal and the first female Cardinal appointed by the Pope – surely the most revolutionary thing he or any of his predecessors had ever done. I certainly felt gratified. I had always wanted a double first.

Fortunately, being descended from the wolf like all dogs, I enjoy rituals and ceremonies which used to play an essential role in keeping the wolf pack orderly, and I still practise a few, like wuffling the Chap's hand at regular intervals to keep the bond between us tight. I think it likely that the reason the Cardinals and other grown men like it too is because ceremonies served a similar purpose when men lived in packs or tribes, as some still do. Of course, vanity is also involved and many men enjoy dressing up as much as women do, the Cardinal's outfit, in particular, being as gaudy as any female garb.

Proud as I was, I inevitably felt inferior because all the other Cardinals had been made in the image of God, even slightly more so, apparently, than ordinary folk, while I was only made in the image of Dog. Nevertheless, with my red Cardinal's collar, my tailored scarlet cassock and the round, tasselled hat, worn only once in life, I thought I looked rather cute, more so than some of my princely colleagues, who were on the fat side.

His Holiness seemed very kind and good though quite a few of his predecessors had not been very holy by all accounts, at least not by canine standards, and by the time he had finished I was a Princess of the Church entitled to be addressed as 'Your Eminence' – not an *éminence grise* but an *éminence chocolat*, though I was not the first in that respect. Most of the other Cardinals went through the motions of welcoming me to their Sacred College, while viewing me with some suspicion as something of an outsider, to say the least. One of them, who was a Franciscan and naturally kind to animals, went out of his way to be especially helpful. However, I felt that a few resented my arrival, sensing that I might upset their comfortable life with my well known revolutionary views concerning the Rights of Dog. There was one Cardinal in particular, a fat Italian, who clearly disliked me, perhaps fearing that one day I might pip him at the post in the race to become the next Pope, which really would be a thrust for feminism and non-discrimination. (In my imaginings my ambition knows no bounds and there is some apocryphal precedent in the form of Pope Joan, a woman said to have occupied the papal chair in the guise of a man *circa* AD 855 and supposed to have disgraced herself by giving birth in the street in Rome, which Pope Dido certainly wouldn't do.) I named my enemy Cardinal 'Bighead' because his head was too large for its contents. He was a man of few words but plenty of black looks and, regarding his eyes, if he had been a dog or a horse you would have turned him down. I just knew in my bones that I was going to cross paws with him.

When I emerged into St Peter's Square after the initiation ceremony all the dogs of Rome seemed to be outside rooting for me, and there are thousands of them. As I was expected to represent the interests of all other animals – the first time in history that this had been possible at such a level – hundreds of cats were there as well, a twenty-four-hour moratorium on the natural conflict between the species having previously been declared, though there were a few minor breaches of the cease-scuffle from time to time. Cats are as resentful as we are at being excluded from paradise, and if donkeys, lambs, camels and other creatures who figure so prominently in the Bible could have made it into the Eternal City they would have been there too. They all regarded me as carrying the torch for them and, obviously, I would have to do something about them all with minimum delay.

As I jumped into one of the long line of chauffeured Cadillacs, provided for us all at somebody's great expense, one wise old mongrel was heard to comment, 'And to think that all this began with a donkey!' It was such a telling remark that I wished I had said it. Naturally for such a unique occasion the world's journalists were waiting to ambush me into making some statement they could misconstrue, no doubt bringing my pups or some other aspect of my sex life into it, while the paparazzi, mamarazzi and pupparazzi had secreted themselves in all manner of extraordinary places, hoping to secure some embarrassing pictures with their zoom lenses. They had already scoured the files of the picture agencies for old photographs showing me naked, some even when I was a pup.

Fortunately, at the risk of being accused of nepotism, I had managed to get the Chap appointed as my adoguensis. As a Cardinal I could not leave Rome without the Pope's permission and I couldn't face long separation from the Chap. Naturally, after fifty years of consorting with journalists he knew how to sort them out.

'Her Eminence is saying nothing at this stage,' he said firmly, leaving the door open for later interviews should these prove useful to my cause.

Then, with the help of the Swiss Guards in their funny uniforms, we were able to make our escape, the paparazzi, in particular, being fearful of those halberds, as though they might have felt them once or twice before.

As I sensed that my reign as a Cardinal might be short, with Bighead certain to intrigue behind the Vatican scenes, I decided to waste no time and to make my pitch at the first opportunity. This turned out to be the next Conclave which had been called to consider, in a leisurely way over three days, various theological matters including the continuing decline in the numbers of active worshippers. I soon learned that if a committee is a gathering of important people who singly can do nothing but together can decide that nothing can be done, then a conclave is a committee with no sense of time whatever. During most of their sterile arguments, some of which have continued over centuries, I stared at Michelangelo's ceiling to see if, among that vast mass of human flesh, there was a single dog. I could not find one, not even among the damned, though eventually I did discover one in a painting of the Last Supper by another artist on the north side wall. It was even smaller than my Jack Russell friend, Charlie. What annoyed me was that there are two quite large cats depicted there!

Eventually, my opportunity to speak arose when we came to discuss the sadly diminishing numbers of our supporters throughout the world. Following the advice of the Chap who is devious, if nothing else, I began my argument in what appeared to be a selfless way.

'Your Holiness, Your Eminences, may I, as someone who by nature can, perhaps, be more objective than it is possible for you to be, make what appears to me to be a fundamental observation. If we are honest with ourselves what we are marketing is paradise and a more certain entry to it than is offered by any other faith. So the question we should ask ourselves is, "Are we marketing our product in the most effective way?" I suggest that the diminishing numbers of practising believers in almost all countries shows that we are not.'

I could see the Pope stirring uneasily on his throne while the Cardinals stared at each other incredulously. Nobody had ever presented the problem in such realistic terms before.

'You may believe that you are closer to heaven than we dogs but we are certainly closer to earth and that is where our immediate problem lies,' I continued. 'So, let us face the fact that we Cardinals are essentially image-makers and if we are to attract millions to our faith we must make paradise not only more credible but more attractive.

'Look above you,' I said, 'at that wonderful ceiling so recently restored at such cost. What do you see? Mountains of human flesh unrelieved by the sight of a single animal. Have you been aware, before now, that all of the creatures so strongly identified with the Christian faith – the lamb, the donkey, Saint Jerome's lion and the doves of peace – are conspicuous by their absence? Yet this is the kind of unbalanced paradise you have been marketing because all animals are barred from it. Yea, even the birds of paradise are denied entry!'

By this time His Holiness was really agitated and some of the Cardinals were obviously waiting for a lead from him to shut me up, but when I am in full voice that is not easy, as our neighbours well know. Perhaps because it was my maiden speech, there was some tradition that it should not be interrupted and the Holy Father did no more than re-position his little white skullcap, an act which may have had some traditional meaning of which I was unaware.

'What was the good of St Francis preaching to the birds if they had no immortal souls?' I asked, at which my little Franciscan friend nodded smilingly only to receive a savage elbow in the ribs from Bighead, sitting next to him. 'With no songbirds in heaven it will not just be Silent Spring but Silent Eternity, save for the chanting of the angelic choirs. No wonder that the angels are always having to sound off on their trumpets, harps and other instruments, just to relieve the monotony. And think of the Heavenly Fields – what good are fields without animals in them? They might as well be deserts, and that's the way they must go without regular animal manure. Ask any conservationist!'

The mere mention of manure in the Sistine Chapel did not go down well.

'Manure! Marketing paradise! That's blasphemy!' I heard Bighead whisper, deliberately loudly, but with nothing to lose I pressed on, knowing that my next point would meet with some approval in view of the Cardinals' traditional reputation for enjoying good food.

'Have you realised that with no animals in paradise you can't even have an egg for your breakfast? Or any milk in your tea? Surely, if the body is resurrected in the form it had in life it has to be fed. Are all the faithful destined to be vegetarians?'

Nobody, not even Bighead, could answer as the question had never been considered.

'And, if we go on believing Genesis, even a vegetarian diet may be denied to you, with no bones for us if we eventually get in,' I continued, warming to my theme. 'If we insist that animals are barred from heaven because they lack immortal souls then there cannot be any trees or plants either because, by the same token, they can't have any souls. So even the vista will be interminably bare and boring.'

The Conclave was shocked into silence as, pointing again to the ceiling, I cried, 'I put it to you that there is nothing more boring than the idea of a place increasingly and eternally filled by naked or night-shirted people, mostly old and ugly, all killing time by talking in an environment totally unrelieved by other, more beautiful creatures. By barring animals we are alienating whole sections of society – the millions of pet lovers, horse lovers and all the conservationists. How do you think all those thousands of twitchers, falconers and pigeon-fanciers react to the thought of an eternity without birds?'

I paused but there was no audible reply, save for angry mumblings.

'Why penalise ourselves when at one stroke we could secure their support and market an altogether more attractive paradise by reinterpreting one little bit of Genesis, as has been done so often with other parts of the Bible? I put it to you that the ancient teaching that dogs and all other animals are totally barred from paradise, however well they have behaved in life and no matter what marvellous services they have performed or what magnificent sacrifices they have made, is long past its sell-by date. So let us make this positive move about the souls of pets now and far more Anglicans will defect to us than they did over the ordination of women!'

I had intended to bang on about the injustice of offering no compensation for the sufferings which so many animals, including some dogs, endure in this world while humans who feel they have had a raw deal here can look forward to eternal happiness, but Bighead could contain himself no longer.

'I must protest,' he cried, rising from his stall with surprising agility for his rotundity. 'This creature, who is not even of our species, comes here telling us what to do with beliefs rooted in thousands of years of history and centuries of critical study and demanding immediate changes of immense theological significance. Has she considered the consequences of allowing animals into paradise? Where would the line be drawn? If dogs and cats are allowed into heaven other deserving creatures could not fairly be barred. Would frogs qualify?' he asked, sarcastically. While I was wondering if he was referring to the French, when I could have had him up for racial as well as species discrimination, he added, 'And snakes?'

'There was a serpent in the Garden of Eden,' I countered, quickly, 'and that was a kind of paradise.'

'That was different,' Bighead said, taken aback. 'The point I am making, as the Bible puts very clearly, is that we humans are set quite apart from the "brutes", which were all specially created for Man – for his use, service and pleasure and to do whatever he likes with them. So there is no way that they could ever have immortal souls. The mere thought of the peace of heaven being sullied by barking dogs is preposterous.'

All the other Cardinals, even my Franciscan, nodded vigorously. I wanted Bighead to explain, if every other living thing had been put on earth solely for Man's use, how he accounted for sharks, tigers, the plague, the Aids virus and the other things which kill him.

'Furthermore,' I retaliated, stung by the nasty reference, 'is the Cardinal aware that his outdated concept of animals as soulless "brutes" has been largely responsible for Man's cruelty to animals which is now condemned throughout the civilised world? It was only in the last century that an Italian Archbishop ruled that, because a dog does not have a soul, it is not sinful to beat it or do anything else with it!'

How was I to know that this Archbishop was one of Bighead's

ancestors, though in theory he was not supposed to have had any children? Flushed like a beetroot, he returned to his tirade.

'As for the egg, Cardinal Dido displayed her profound theological ignorance in thinking that any of us will ever feel hungry in paradise, where intellectual bliss will eliminate all physical appetites.'

'That will make it duller than ever,' I ventured, while noting that Bighead might be making a rash assumption in believing that he would be there at all. 'No breaks for meals! It's no coincidence that the Moslem faith is increasing while it promises not only food and wine in paradise but sex!'

That did it and I realised I had overcooked my case as the Conclave agreed, overwhelmingly, to move on to other matters. Stupidly, in my anger and frustration, I went still further over the top by suggesting that the Vatican should change its name to Vatican't and the Sacred College to the Scared College, but what really bugged them all was when I then insisted on saying 'Adogs' instead of 'Amen' every time that word arose, as it does so often in Church affairs. That really blew it.

Suddenly scores of scarlet pates were bobbing about the Pope's white one and Bighead emerged from the scrum with a cry of. 'That dog must be extirpated from our midst without further delay. She is the Devil in disguise. I suspected it the moment I saw her tail. No self-respecting Cardinal should have a tail. Examine it to see if it has a barb at the end!'

Not even the Pope was open to my pleas. Bell, Book and Candle were solemnly sent for. The Candle was enormous and, with Bighead wielding it, I was so sure that he was going to hit me on the head with it that I head-butted him first and the impact woke me up, shivering the way I do when I go to the vet.

The experience, fantasy though it was, has convinced me that my chances of making the necessary changes through any Church authority are zilch. So, not being prepared to give up the fight for the right to paradise of dog and other worthy creatures, I will create my own religious outfit. I will set myself up as a guru, claiming direct access to the heavenly powers. After all, if the truth can be spiritually revealed to a man, as gurus claim, why not to a dog if we are all God's creatures? Furthermore, I am in no doubt that Labradors are the chosen race, fated to point out that the dogma that the whole of Nature was created for Man's use is having catastrophic effects by sanctioning his instinct to exploit everything, living and inanimate, without thought for the future, with all the horrible results the world is already witnessing.

So here's looking forward to plenty of rich sponsors and gullible disciples who will set me up, not only with a propaganda platform, but with lots of mansions and Rolls-Royces, which are even more prestigious than Cadillacs.

CHAPTER 15
Psycho-Dido

We had all been watching a TV programme about an American scientist who believes in psychokinesis, that is the power of human thought to influence the movement of a physical object, sometimes referred to as the power of mind over matter. He had designed machines which, he believes, can be affected by people staring at them and willing them to behave in a certain manner. Years previously, other scientists had claimed to be able to affect the way that dice fell when shaken out of a cup. The results of such experiments were usually only marginally in favour of the mental force, whatever it might be, but believers think that they are caused by a capability of the human mind which is only just developing and, therefore, is not very strong but will become very important in the future as the brain increases its capacity.

Inevitably the Chap, who was trained as a scientist, airily dismissed all the results as 'statistical quirks', but I was not so sure. I fell to thinking that perhaps the power of the human mind over matter is really a left over from the days of primitive man, when it was much stronger and more important and has since waned through disuse. In that case, we dogs might still possess it because our brains are supposed to be primitive compared with human brains, and therefore nearer to primitive man's. We may still have something in our brains that yours have dispensed with in the course of evolution. After all, we are supposed to possess extra senses, such as telepathy with our masters, which enable us to know when they are returning from long distances, and there is also our remarkable ability to find our way home over terrain previously unknown to us, which human beings entirely lack, the feats of some of my species being quite astounding. While the ability to influence inanimate objects seems more far-fetched nobody has ever tested dogs for it. Perhaps we could do the willing more strongly than humans if only we were given a chance.

It's a funny thing how watching TV is so soporific. Suddenly I was with the Chap, in my yellow collar and on my yellow lead, wandering round the fairground at a fête which I had opened, as I am regularly asked to do as a VID. On these occasions the Chap would like to get away as quickly as possible after I have done my act but, for appearances' and consciences' sake, mine as well as his, he feels obliged to go round the charity stalls and buy a few cheap things and then have a go on one or two of the fairground amusements. So there we were at a stand which had a big horizontal pointer, like the hand of an enormous clock, which was set in motion and then eventually stopped at a number. Whoever had the ticket corresponding to that number won the prize. With the power of mind over matter fresh in my brain, I fell to staring at twenty-four, the number on the Chap's ticket, concentrating really hard, and, sure enough, the pointer stopped just where I wanted it to. The Chap's prize was a set of aluminium pots and pans and, feeling a bit guilty for having won it in front of so many people, he felt that he must fork out for another go, being certain that, by the laws of chance, he was most unlikely to win again. This time his number was sixty-nine and I stared really hard at it. Up it came, making the Chap the recipient of a rather appalling giant pink teddy bear. As he hastily offloaded this on to the nearest small girl he was urged by the crowd to 'do the hat-trick', which is exactly what he did, winning one of those adjustable American hats with an enormous peak.

By now, hooked on his winning streak, wearing his peaked hat and with a large crowd gathering, he continued, winning in succession a giant panda, a Paddington bear, a silly dog called Goofy, to which I rather took exception, and a dreadful-looking doll. Each time his number came up the crowd cheered though I suspect that those who continued to lose their money began to think it must be a fiddle, especially when the pointer stopped at his number with something of a shudder. Eventually, after twelve straight wins, the Chap was too embarrassed to continue though I wanted him to go on because I felt certain that somehow I was affecting that pointer. So much so that I reckoned that the prizes, or at least half of them, belonged to me. I could have had a lot of fun ripping up that dreadful teddy bear.

Of course, the Chap put it all down to chance – tossed coins may come down heads a dozen times on the trot and somebody always wins the National Lottery against astronomical odds. He was willing to concede that I might have brought him luck, as everyone was suggesting, but I could not wait for another opportunity to test out my belief that I possessed the mysterious force in a big way. I had, in fact, suspected for a long time that the Chap's reputation as a successful trout fisherman owed a lot to my presence by his side on the river, when I will the trout to take his fly. He has often remarked that I bring him luck but without asking himself why, as a scientist should.

A few days later I got my chance when the Boss was playing snakes and ladders with some visiting grandchildren. They thought I was just watching but I was doing more than that. I found that I could will the dice to come down on any number I chose by staring hard at it. Every time the Boss needed a six up it came and up the ladder she went. Whatever number she wanted I produced yet, when I looked away and didn't stare, everything was random and she went down her fair share of snakes.

It was the smallest of the grandchildren, Phillipa, who put three and three together every time I willed a six. She ran and told the Chap to take me away because I was bringing her bad luck! He then remembered the fairground episode, came to watch and was amazed as, time after time, I produced numbers on the rolling dice to order, looking at him with my well-known smile every time I did so. He was so amazed, in fact, that he could not wait to go to a big toyshop in London and buy the best roulette wheel he could find.

I quickly cottoned on to the requirement as he spun the wheel and set the little ball in motion in the privacy of the floor in his locked study. Making the ball fall into black or red was a doddle, and after achieving one hundred per cent success in fifty tries he was clearly excited. He then started backing specific numbers and, provided I concentrated really hard, the ball went into the right channel every time. I suppose that the Chap could have written a newspaper article about it there and then and organised a display of my extraordinary power on television, but I fear that greed had reared its ugly nut. He claimed that he needed further proof, but I know he had seen a chance of some easy money.

He reached for the telephone and rang up John Aspinall, better known as 'Aspers', owner of the famous Howletts Zoo in Kent and proprietor of a gambling club in London. The Chap had met him a few times and they shared a common interest in zoology.

'I wonder if you would do me a favour,' he said, as casually as he could. 'I am writing a novel which involves roulette in a casino. I know nothing about it and I need to see it in action and, perhaps, make a few small stakes so that I can experience the atmosphere and the feel of it all. Would you be kind enough to let me do that in your club?'

After so many years in journalism the Chap can be very persuasive over the telephone but I can tell by looking at his face when he is trying to pull a fast one – as he claims he can tell from mine. Having secured permission and fixed a date he then raised the problem point.

'There's just one slight snag, Aspers. I shall be up in London signing books at a bookshop with my dog Dido, the authoress whom I'm sure you've heard about. I daren't leave her in a car parked in London these days and it may be too hot to do that safely anyway. Could I take her in with me? She'll sit very quietly and we shan't be there long.'

Whatever Aspers might have thought, his love of animals is so great that he gave his permission.

'Now we shall really see!' the Chap said to me as he put down the telephone. It was a triumph for brass nerve which, as a private nose myself, I quite admire. I wouldn't like a cowed Chap any more than he would like a cowed dog.

The gambling room was very impressive with lush fittings and thick carpets though, understandably, not very full on the afternoon when we went there. The pretty girl croupier made a great fuss of me. Fortunately she had read the paperback of my first book which shows me sitting, rather grandly, on a chair and, with a little ingenious prodding from the Chap, she offered me a seat where I could watch the proceedings. It was just as well because, while I might think hard about the Chap's number if he called it out, I thought that I really needed to concentrate my force on the little ball and keep my eye on it.

Obviously confident in my ability, the Chap began to bet on numbers right away. Perhaps it would have been more clever if we had arranged to lose occasionally, but we hadn't and every time we won the croupier and others on the staff who came to watch looked more and more puzzled. They were used to the occasional run of luck by professional gamblers but they sensed that this was something different and the higher the Chap's piles of chips grew the less they liked the look of it. While the croupier had joked about the intensity with which I was watching the ball, following it with my eyes, she soon became suspicious of it and, being superstitious, like most people connected with gambling, was sure that I was bringing the Chap an undue quota of luck. Anyway, she made an excuse to deprive me of my seat by offering it to one of the lady spectators. When I could no longer see the ball the Chap began to experience his share of failures. Completely convinced that I possessed the force, he quit, cashed his chips and found himself £60,000 better off thanks to my efforts. The smile on his face as we walked back to our parked car was an unforgettable expression of the ineffable joy of something for nothing, which seems to mean so much to humans while we expect it all the time. Frankly, I thought the money belonged to me and should have gone into my royalties account at Lloyds Bank on the time-honoured female principle that what's his is mine and what's mine is my own but, apart from the odd extra treat, I got no share of it.

Having established my power of mind over matter, the next big question was what were we going to do about it?

'It would be great to fly to Monte Carlo and break the bank but they'd never let you in,' the Chap remarked to me on the drive back home.

Nor, I thought, would they let me back into the UK without six months' quarantine, thank you very much!

'I think we should keep quiet until we can arrange a nationwide demonstration on TV with full scientific control,' he finally thought aloud.

It was a great idea but he had reckoned without the gambling grapevine. Mayfair was soon buzzing with the news that a well-known bitch had beaten the bank at a casino and that I was she. By the time we reached home the telephones were ringing for interviews by the media. The Chap declined to say anything that day but, nevertheless, next morning's papers were full of the story. Did Dog Rig Roulette Wheel? was typical, the editors having taken the view that under British law a dog cannot be libelled. When Aspers had been asked for a quote he had unwittingly fed the speculation by saying: 'In my experience anything is possible with animals. If a dog can do that what could a gorilla do?'

There was no difficulty whatever in setting up the TV demonstration, for which all the channels were competing. While leading scientists declined to sully their reputations by being even remotely associated with such an unlikely story, the Chap managed to recruit a distinguished animal psychologist to set up and oversee dice and roulette experiments. With most of the nation watching after the publicity build-up I achieved scores close to one hundred per cent. The newspapers could no longer be denied their interviews and, to the great annoyance of all the politicians and showbiz stars, I dominated the front pages of even the 'quality' newspapers.

Various 'experts' writing for the press insisted that it must be a clever conjuring trick and accused the Chap of being an accessory, which was quite a joke because he hadn't a clue how I did it. They were not convinced even when I demonstrated that I could do it when the Chap wasn't present. Inevitably, the biggest sceptics were the scientists. Publicly they ignored the irrefutable evidence but behind the scenes at the Royal Society and elsewhere there was panic. That the sacred laws of motion and mechanics propounded by Sir Isaac Newton and fortified by 300 years of research and application should be undermined by a dog seemed preposterous and, to use the in-word, unacceptable. Tabloid newspapers, which seem to think all scientists are crazy, came up with 'Dog Makes Scientists Mad', the *Sun* coming up to scratch with 'Dog Addles Egg-heads'.

The Chap's offer to make me available for any tests they cared to contrive was ignored by the scientists as beneath their dignity. Instead, there were unscientific mutterings like 'Something will have to be done about that dog', but, on the face of things, eliminating me would achieve nothing because it should follow that if I possessed the force so might every other dog. This, of course, was not lost on other dog owners and the shops experienced a run on dice and toy roulette wheels, but nobody came up with a candidate so it looked as though I might be a one-off though my own view was that the other dogs were not bright enough to realise what they were supposed to do.

The public which, by and large, loves to believe in magic were on my side, which rattled the scientists still further. No dog had ever caused such chaos and I was loving it! My only regret was that it created a field day for the occultologists who claimed that I had finally proved that anything was possible. The astrologers argued that if a living brain can influence the behaviour of a small ball then a huge ball, like a planet, must be able to influence the behaviour of the living brain. Millions of their followers lapped it up and their trade in phone-in horoscopes peaked. The 'Flying Saucer' enthusiasts claimed that it was clear that if I could influence the movement of a dice or ball I could do the same to an apple falling from a tree. I was, therefore, an anti-gravity machine, proving that such a force did exist, as they had always insisted. The only concession they made was that flying saucers were probably not crewed by little green men, as previously believed, but by little green dogs. This was no surprise to me as I have always maintained that all those mysterious corn circles are probably made by very large extra-terrestrial dogs going round and round, as all dogs do before they settle. Those who believed in levitation latched on to my achievement as did the theologians, who claimed that what I had really performed was a miracle because the definition of a miracle is an event which defies the laws of nature. So, what I had done was clear proof of the existence of miracles and if one miracle is possible then any are. Furthermore, certain bishops argued that if a mere dog could cause nature's laws to be set aside, it should be no surprise that saints could work such wonders!

There was widespread newspaper speculation about my financial value and the Chap was deluged with offers to buy me, the largest coming from certain Arab sheikhs, well-known in the casinos. When he publicly declared that he would never part with me at any price we were concerned about the danger of my being dognapped, but what was most disturbing was the interest of the Ministry of Defence which made the Chap fear that we might be silenced under the Official Secrets Act. According to cryptic messages which the Chap received through mysterious intermediaries some defence scientists thought that I might be able to interfere with microelectronic switches, in which case a team of a hundred trained dogs might have the power to disrupt the computers which control most weapons these days and ruin their operations. What a turn-up! In the past military leaders had enlisted the mystical aid of gods in battle. Now it seemed that dogs might be a better bet!

The demands for our services were so great that, in desperation, the Chap suspended all communications and took me down to our private stretch of the river to fish and get some peace. It turned out to be an unwise move because forces even more sinister than the Ministry of Defence were being secretly mustered against me. If the Cold War had still been in progress the Chap and I would have been on our guard against the KGB, in view of the military implications, especially as the Russians are supposed to have been deeply interested in 'psychic warfare'. The Chap had already raised the fear in my mind by wondering if I would be equally effective in influencing the outcome of Russian roulette, but the spectre of being dognapped by the KGB had receded. So, I felt it reasonably safe to mooch along the riverbank in my usual places.

As I did so my collar was suddenly grabbed by a burly thug while another, equally as tough-looking, slipped on a lead and dragged me away to a waiting car with dark windows. It was quickly clear that my captors were not only Americans but had particularly rich accents. My Dog! I thought, I've been dognapped by the CIA! I had given tongue as soon as I had been seized but the Chap was out of bark-shot because he was fishing near a noisy sluice. Sure that I would be flown out to CIA headquarters, outside Washington, I began to doubt that I would ever see the Chap or the Boss again.

I sensed that we were racing down the M4 to London and, sure enough, I soon found myself in a flat in South Audley Street. Without delay I was lifted into the bath and dyed black which convinced me that my captivity was going to be permanent. The person who did the dyeing was a woman, called Dolly, whose own hair showed that she was well used to undergoing the process herself which, perhaps, induced her to handle me more gently than her male companions had done. Though she looked hard-boiled and sounded ill-educated, like her colleagues, I felt that Dolly was a dog lover, as any dog can immediately detect.

As soon as I was dry my captors, known to each other, respectively, as Al and Joe, and who, true to form, smoked big cigars and wore gold rings, took me into the living room where there was a full-size roulette wheel on the table. I was lifted on to a chair and it was clear, from the professional way they set the ball in motion, they had played before.

'Right, Doodah, twenty-eight!' Al commanded, as they all looked at me expectantly.

Of course, I didn't try an inch, especially when he couldn't even get my name right, and the ball slid into number six.

'Now see here, stoopid pooch,' Al said, menacingly, 'you concentrate your goddamn eyes on that goddamn ball . . . or else! Fifteen!'

I looked hard at the ball but fixed my gaze on channel number fourteen, where the ball duly entered.

'Give her a chance. She's only one off!' Dolly said, as Joe removed his belt and laid it on the table.

'Right! Twelve!' Al cried.

I made sure that the ball went into number twenty-one.

'Wrong way round, you dope!' Joe yelled, as he held the belt in front of my nose, menacingly.

By now I was sure that they were not CIA men after all but mobsters who wanted to use me for gambling purposes. Clearly, if I continued to fail they would not bother to take me to America and, whatever else they might do to me, I would avoid that.

'Let me try,' Dolly said. 'I guess Dido doesn't respond to threats. Now come on, Dido! Zero! Just for me.'

Following abject failure after failure all three soon lost their patience.

'We are wasting our goddamn time and the Chief's money,' Al said, finally. 'Better ring Las Vegas and cut our losses.'

There was a brief telephone conversation with the Chief, who seemed a man of few words. 'OK,' I heard him say, 'we've been taken for a ride and that's what you do with that dawg. Get the next plane back.'

They consulted the airlines and found that, if they moved fast, they could leave that evening. The hoods decided that they had no time to deal with me but would just turn me loose on the airport car park when they handed back their hired car. Dolly, bless her, had other ideas. It was she who was detailed to push me out of the car while the men dealt with the luggage. Not only did she leave me inside it and put on my own collar, which she had brought in her handbag, but, at the last minute, told one of the airline girls that I was there. Soon, I was in the hands of the airport police who knew who I must be, in spite of my colour, when they read my collar tag and tried the telephone number, which the Chap answered.

Both the Chap and the Boss raced to the airport to pick me up and the exuberance of their joy at seeing me was so great that it woke me up. The whole adventure had been a daymare, but it taught me a couple of things about real life. To be an exceptional individual in this world entails an intolerable amount of hassle and no little danger. And all those credulous human weirdies really are out there just waiting for someone like me to surface.

CHAPTER 16
Shot at Dawn

Most females dream of being a star in the film world and I am no exception, but most of all I wanted to be a director because of the sense of power it would give me. The Chap had also been negotiating unsuccessfully for a film based on my books. So, with this mix of desire and frustration strong in my mind, it was small wonder that I fell into a reverie about it. The charm of reveries is that all real-life difficulties can be resolved at a stroke.

Being determined to stage a village film I decided to start my new career with a straightforward project with no spurious claims to profundity: an all-dog Western. After all, we live in West Berkshire, conveniently near 'state' borders with Wiltshire and Hampshire over which outlaws can escape, and the Western is as much part of common fantasy here as it is in America, where it never really happened either. As for being the director it was my camcorder we would be using and I would also be putting up the first tranche of the money – an investment of fifty pounds from my book royalties – so, whether they liked it or not, all those taking part would have to do as I wished, with me telling them exactly how from my canvas chair, which would have DIDO in large letters on the back. (I wonder why, in my day-dreams, I am always exerting naked power. Perhaps it is because in real life, with the Chap believing he is the pack leader, I have to disguise it, which I think I do rather successfully.)

I am prepared to do a lot for the village but fear I can operate only as a one-dog band, being allergic to committees or any other arrangement that allows individuals to drone on for the sake of it. Nor can I stand it when others, whether dogs or people, try to get in on my act when I've generated all the bright ideas and done all the slog. You have to work on a village project to appreciate all the back-biting and petty jealousies. Talk about prima doggas!

I thought deeply about the basic requirements for a successful Western and listed them on the notepaper on my clipboard. The first was cowboys and, from comments by the Chap when he has had odd jobs done on the house, there were plenty of those around. It is odd, isn't it, how the word 'cowboy' is romantic while 'cowman' is the reverse. It is hard to imagine anyone less exciting than a cowman, who wouldn't even have done for Lady Chatterley's lover. Yet cowboys must have been every bit as ordinary and smelly as cowmen and no better looking on average. I suppose the same applies to cowdogs, which would be a term I would have to avoid, cowbitches being even worse. Cowboys are also prone to use their fists, which cowmen are not noted for, but paw and jaw fights – usually more noise than anything else – are second nature to the males of our species so there should be no difficulty there. Of course, we would need broad-brimmed hats, even if the weather was dull, black ones for the baddies and light-coloured ones for the goodies, who would always have to win. I had always thought it odd that even when struck on the jaw and sent flying a cowboy usually manages to keep his hat on. I made a note to find out how that was done. My own hat, as director, would be a baseball cap borrowed from the Chap's grandson only, unlike him, I would not wear it back to front.

Like every good dream, every good Western should have at least one chase in it, preferably more. This is usually done on horseback with one of the contesting groups being called a posse. My immediate problem would be a supply of horses, apart from the difficulty which dogs would experience in riding them. Kintbury used to be called a one-horse village but the horse had died and, while we had Lambourn, Highclere Castle and other racing establishments close by, I couldn't see any owners lending me their thoroughbreds for a village film. There are also a couple of nice nags which pull the show boat on the canal but they are carthorses and dogs would look silly on them. In fact, dogs on any horses would convey the atmosphere of a circus rather than a rodeo. With funds too low to hire horses for any purpose we might have to settle for the noise of their hooves made with the empty halves of coconuts, at the wielding of which the Chap claims to be dexterous from his theatrical days in his youth. We would probably have to economise in other ways on sound effects, using my coyote howl for instance, the veracity of this being familiar to all our neighbours. Anyway, such details could wait.

A stagecoach, with some tough-looking dog riding shotgun, would lend verisimilitude to the scene, but the nearest things on offer were the pony and trap which carries the May Queen and a donkey and trap which appears on other occasions. I felt that even with Wells Farrago or some other nonsense painted on them by the village signwriter they would still not carry conviction, though with a fifty-quid budget (the Chap is mean with the joint account, always being worried about a rainy day) everything and everybody might have to be pressed into service. Perhaps we could borrow a wagon train from the former Littlecote theme park. I would have to work on the owner there, Peter de Savaloy, whom I see at intervals. Whatever it took, I was determined to do a really professional job, as with everything else I do.

The third requirement would be guns with lots of good reasons for using them. I realised that, while guns would have to be flourished, the climax would be a stare-out rather than a shoot-out because, by and large, we dogs do not like to hurt each other, at least not seriously, because that would make no biological sense. Only humans are daft enough to kill each other and I wanted our picture to project the right message in these violent times. In any canine skirmish one dog will eventually submit and the most that would be lost would be an ear, which is dispensible while life isn't. Though plenty of guns would have to be on view they would have to be replicas because of the tough gun laws prevailing in these parts after the local real-life massacre two miles from us in Hungerford. I was sure that I could borrow plenty from the local children but, until they arrived, and with the cast needing a lot of practice, they would have to improvise by using bananas. After all, no live bullets are ever fired in a Western which is why nobody worries about ricochets. The whole thing is sheer make-believe, which is what a good director does – make people believe it.

Finally we would need a quiet location and our area was ideally suited. There are plenty of prairies – hedgeless fields once laid down to wheat and now in 'set-aside' and stretching for miles. Good Westerns are usually based on battles over territory and nobody is more sensitive about territory than dogs. There are no Red Indians in these parts, though we have some brown ones, and there are plenty of vandals I would like to see put away on reservations. There are lots of cattle too, of which, no doubt, some are mavericks, though whether we would be allowed to stage round-ups I would have to discover. A stampede scene seemed even less likely to gain support but I would try the local farmers at the undignified risk of getting the bum's rush. Anything for the village!

As for 'cow towns' there were Oxford and Bulford fairly close by and, as many residents would agree, Kintbury itself would qualify as the most infamous of all, Dog City. The Kennet could be the Rio Grande or, with clever photography under my direction, we could even press the canal into service, perhaps with some rather optimistic prospectors panning for gold there. We even have the railway – sorry, railroad – within a couple of hundred yards.

To supply further local colour, there are plenty of saloons close by to justify such visualisations as 'A bunch of the boys are whooping it up in the Blue Ball saloon . . .' There is even one, not far away, called the Klondike! With a suitable sign outside, our own house might make a good one, if the Boss would play. With my preference for anything to do with food we could call it the Golden Nougat. There should be no difficulty in finding a few canine floosies to stand around in the saloons topless, as we always are anyway, because I fancied a few steamy scenes, though it would not do for a village film to be a collar-ripper. As for lone rangers, there are always a few about in the form of stray dogs from other villages, and we could fit one of them up with a mask.

We have a very convenient Post Office which could stand in as a bank to be robbed, as the video shop next door actually was recently, by armed bandits. Then, right next door to us, we have 'Boot Hill', the churchyard where we could go through the motions of burying any fallen gunslingers with reverence, if the vicar would allow it. Unaccompanied dogs are not allowed in the churchyard and there was no way that we could film a burial with dogs on leads. That would look ridiculous. I would have to work on our lady vicar, who is a good friend of mine.

With such matters settled in my mind, the plot and the script more or less wrote themselves, my working title being *The Shoot-Out at KS Corral*, KS standing for Kintbury Square, but as I would be changing the story as I went, like all good directors, the eventual title would be different, perhaps *High Moon* if I decided to shoot the climax at night when there would be nobody else about. The script would, of course, have to be peppered with immortal lines such as 'This square ain't big enough for you and me', 'Make my day', and, especially, 'Well, I'll be dog-gone!' while one of the bitches would have to utter 'Diamonds are a dog's best friend'. There would also be a good smattering of words like 'pardner', 'gringo' and 'old timer'. I had already devised a brilliantly innovative idea for connecting various sequences. I would simply cut when convenient and the words 'Meanwhile, back at the ranch . . .' would appear on the screen.

Casting the film presented the usual problems which all directors face though, being female, I was spared the need for a casting couch. I would have liked an all-Labrador cast but that would have laid me open to a charge of discrimination and, perhaps, made the film too bland. Charlie, the scarred and weather-beaten Jack Russell with the lived-in face, was tailor-made for Wotta Twerp, the former gunfighter turned marshal, and would have to be in the film anyway because he's never away from the square and, if left out, could be guaranteed to be a spoiler. There is a little Yorkshire terrier that would also have to be given a part to keep the village peace, though I had to watch that I didn't end up with a cast of midgets. Corrib, a glossy black Labrador friend of mine, would make a good Dog Holliday while a nice golden retriever, called Monty, could be another gunfighter. I also jotted down a black flat-coated Retriever called Will, who is also a fishing pal. I intended to have as many famous and infamous gunslingers as possible in the cast, irrespective of historic accuracy, dogs like Messey James, Bat Masterpup and Wild Bill Hiccup. The Yorkshire terrier could play Billy the Kid, which was just a walk-on part, and we could also bring in the Sundance Kid if the weather was right. I would recruit my chocolate son, Charlton (no relation to Heston), who lives locally, for the part of the hero Wild Bill Hiccup, and another son, amusingly called Pincher, a name with which I could have a lot of fun. I think I would cast Pincher as Jasper, the crooked saloon owner, or perhaps the bent judge. I might be accused of nepotism but what the hell! For the ritual Chinese cook, operating the chuck wagon, we could borrow a Peke from a local takeaway, provided they haven't eaten it.

Red Indians were going to be a problem because in any Western I ever make they will get a fair deal and not be made fun of and mowed down as they usually are. I like Red Indians because they had such a wonderful attitude to dogs and other animals, their concept of the next world being more civilised than most. Every Indian was sure that animals were as entitled to life as he was, both taking their chances in the tough struggle for survival and going to paradise when they died, and that in particular a man would meet up with his dog there. So I would just have a few for local colour, sitting around a wigwam making smoke signals, but not to be massacred. Indeed I feel so strongly about massacres that if I found, as we went along, that I must have one, I would make it Custard's Last Stand. Crazy Dog, chief of the savage Blackpaws, would be suitable for just sitting around, smoking a pipe of peace. Charlie would have fitted the title and had the right coloured paws but I had already cast him as Twerp. If driven to it, I should have no difficulty in finding a Sitting Bull Terrier instead. Or, I could offer the part to a Norfolk terrier called Snuff who stays with me occasionally though, being hyperactive, he is not very good at sitting, and Jumping Bull doesn't sound right.

As for the floosies, I could think of several candidates for Dog Holliday's girlfriend, who was known as Big Nose Kate and was a real dog-eater. My chocolate Labrador friend Amber, who is very eloquent with body language, lives in Scotland but would, no doubt, journey down for such a star part. Calamity Jane and Diamond Lil were further musts. I would need to find a husky for the part of Eskimo Nell but Dead-Eyed Dick should pose no difficulty among the males in these parts.

There came the moment when we had to make a decision about the horse problem because the coconuts, while useful, would obviously not be enough. Oddly, it was Charlie who came up with the idea which seemed so clever at the time.

'Why don't we complete the illusion by spreading a lot of manure about to show where the horses have been and gone?' he suggested.

'Brilliant! I like it,' I responded. 'We should be able to get a cartload from Lambourn.'

'That would be no good,' Charlie replied, being knowledgeable about most local matters through his incessant wanderings in which he sniffs into every nook and cranny. 'Their manure's all mixed with the news-paper they use these days for the horses' bedding, and *I'm* not going to separate it.'

Neither am I, I thought, and to use it as it was would be an anachronism which would ruin the picture, especially as some bits of newspaper might have dates on them. Of course, Hollywood avoids the problem by never having any manure of any kind on the set, even though there may be hundreds of horses. I suppose they must have men handy with buckets and shovels, which is cheating in my book. We would put that right and it would save us a lot of money provided nobody slipped in it and sued for compensation, which everybody seems to be doing these days.

'Where can we get some that hasn't got paper in it?' I asked.

'I know where there's plenty lying right handy,' Charlie replied. 'On the rhubarb in the allotments.'

'Right,' I said, making a note on my pad, for the allotments are just a bone's throw from the square. 'Horse manure is down to you and get plenty – as much as possible, at first light on the morning when we shoot the square scenes. Spread it around generously to intensify the illusion in the mind of the audience, for the larger the pile of manure the bigger the posse that has just ridden by.'

I also made a note to get more coconuts as the Chap would never be able to cope alone with so many imaginary hooves.

Charlie's determination in all matters lead to an hilarious scene which did not amuse me at the time. While I was taking a gentle stroll round the allotments, wondering how to cope with a demand from certain members of the cast for stand-ins for the dangerous sequences, I saw him shooting repeatedly with his banana into a huge pile of cow manure.

'What on earth are you doing?' I asked.

'I'm practising shooting crap.'

'Idiot!' I cried. 'Shooting crap is throwing dice!'

We soon ran short of money, the budget-buster being the cost of camcorder cassette refills because I had to make so many re-takes. I asked the Chap for permission to withdraw more from our joint account at Lloyds Bank in Hungerford, but he refused saying, 'You'll just be throwing good money after bad.' I was annoyed but could hardly approach him again at that stage, having just seen the rushes of a brief sequence in which I had placed such high hopes. It was a scene in which a half-breed cowboy is sent by Twerp to size up and report back on a mysterious stranger who looked like a gunfighter and was holed up, suspiciously, in one of the saloons, having just hit town. This spy was supposed to return to Twerp's office with a one-line report so brilliantly succinct that it said everything:

'He wears one, low, like he knows how.' Out of the goodness of my heart I had given the part to a mongrel who had just come to live in the village from the north of England and it was all he had to say but, in repeat after repeat, he kept on making the most unholy hash of it. His trouble was that in the north they use 'like' as we use 'you know', and he simply could not stop himself from saying 'He wears one low, like. He knows how,' which ruined what I thought was the best line in the script. No wonder we needed so many camcorder cassettes!

In my wily way I had also inserted that line to convince the cast that a professional gunfighter only used one gun because they had all started agitating for two and we couldn't raise them. It would also have meant providing a double ration of bananas for practice. As it was, they already kept demanding more bananas claiming that they were getting too ripe for use when I suspected they were eating them. I made a note to supply very green bananas in any future film I might direct.

'We need an angel,' I said to the cast, despondently, realising that we were on our uppers, a phrase which made sense to those of the cowboys and cowgirls who were wearing boots.

'The vicar's always banging on about angels,' the Yorkshire terrier volunteered. 'Why not get her to intervene?'

'Not that kind of angel, you little ass,' I said, wearily. 'In our profession an angel is a backer, someone who puts up money as an investment in a show. I'm thinking of somebody like Sir Andrew Lloyd-Webfoot.'

Sir Andrew, who has produced several highly successful shows, lives close by and is rather a duckie. I see him from time to time and, as one of his winners was called *Cats*, I had even written to him suggesting a sequel called 'Dogs', but without response.

The Wednesday morning which I had selected for shooting the main scenes in the square dawned fine and clear. We were due to start at five a.m. knowing that provided we were through by seven-thirty we should not be interrupted as nobody gets up early at our end of the village. When I stepped outside the house I faced two severe shocks. The first was the sight of all the wheelie-bins. I had forgotten that the dustmen come on Wednesday and that everyone puts their wheelie-bin out on Tuesday night. They all had to be removed and hidden away, which wasted a lot of time. The second was the enormous amount of manure that Charlie had managed to scatter all over the square. I had told him to put out as much as possible but, clearly, there had been far more rhubarb on those allotments than I had appreciated and I realised that I should have made a reconnaissance. With the dustmen expected any time after eight a.m. there was no time to remove it. When the gunmen made their long, slow walk towards each other for their personal showdown they would just have to pick their way through the heaps. At least it would be different, I consoled myself.

There were a few other, more minor problems to resolve before I could reach that spine-tingling moment and cry through my megaphone 'And action!' to be followed by the continuity dog coming in with the clapper-board shouting 'Take One'. In true Charlie fashion, Twerp turned up wearing an eye-patch which made him look more like a pirate than a cowboy, and Big Nose Kate had so grossly over used the make-up that she looked like a clown, though, oddly, that is fashionable for women these days.

I thought they all looked an awful rag and bobtail lot but, wasting no more time, I began to direct the slow walk to the shoot-out between Wotta Twerp and the Sundance Kid, who was played by a big half-breed dog. Naturally, to satisfy human audience requirements, the little guy had to win but the two contestants were so overanxious not to get their boots dirty that they picked their way through the steaming manurial heaps with such excessive care that they bumped into each other. Charlie then made a hash of getting his gun out, in spite of all his practice at being quick on the draw with his banana, and the Sundance Kid fired the only shot. Because of the unpleasant consequences neither was prepared to fall to the ground and I had to cut and re-run the whole sequence after calling for shovels to clear a space for the Sundance Kid to die in.

Charlie distinguished himself further in the final corral gunfight, with the baddies firing from behind the low churchyard wall, only the crown of their hats and their guns showing. The child's Wellingtons, which Charlie had borrowed and insisted on wearing, were so big that he was too small for his boots, one of which became embedded in a heap of manure. Still firing away, as he imagined Twerp would have done in such an emergency, he looked ridiculous as he shook the trapped boot off and immediately trod in the next heap. Billy the Kid was so small that he was using the heaps for cover while Dog Holliday was also out of camera because he persisted in taking so much cover that nobody could see him. When I cast him I had not known that he was gun-shy, as some Labradors are.

I kept calling 'cut' but nobody took any notice, pretending not to hear me. The whole episode had degenerated into a shambles and there was worse to come. I looked up the street and there, turning into it, was the huge dustcart which had arrived earlier than usual. Seeing no bins, the dustmen walked down on to the set amazed by the quantity of manure. There was talk of strike action but I managed to induce them to do the rest of the village first and come back later by which time, I promised, the wheelies would be back in place and the street cleared. They gave me fifteen minutes.

We had completely run out of time and there was no chance of a re-take of the shoot-out, which is what the film was really all about. We had also run out of money. Gone were my hopes of an Oscar or a showing at the Cannes Film Festival or of having my pawprints in the concrete outside that movie-house in Hollywood. To recoup my investment I was already toying with the degrading prospect of selling the video to Jeremy Beagle, but there then occurred one of those chance events which tend to intrude into the lives of dogs of destiny.

I had barely got rid of the dustmen when a car pulled up outside the baker's, which always opens early, and who should alight from it but Sir Andrew Lloyd-Webfoot, who was collecting the bread as his wife was out riding. Seeing this as the intervention of Fate, with the big loaf of bread in his hand reminding me about what happens if you cast it on the waters – the ducks eat it – I decided to cut my losses and seek advice from a true professional.

'Do you think it would make a musical?' I asked, after I had briefly explained the project, not only hoping that he would write the music but back it as well. (As the Boss says, you never get anywhere without brass nerve.) I could not hear the answer plainly because Sir Andrew was holding his nose. Though used to horses, his nostrils had never been assailed in quite such a concentrated manner, even though most of the offending material was back on the rhubarb.

'Send me the video,' he said, nasally, clearly anxious to make his escape.

I duly did so and, as I later learned, he played it to his house guests who fell about in fits of laughter at what they judged to be a brilliantly hilarious send-up of village life. This was not what I had intended at all but when Sir Andrew offered to market the video as a comedy through one of his companies I swallowed my pride, if only because there is little that gives me greater pleasure than proving the Chap wrong.

'Throwing good money after bad' was it? I would see to it, this time, that my royalties were paid into a different account to which only I would have access. Then once I had some capital I could go for more serious projects such as a film I had in mind about Dracula to be called *The Vampire's Decision is Final*, in which there would be no need for horses. Or I might do a British version of *The Hunchback of Notre Dame* because our church is also dedicated to Our Lady and there are some whacking great bells in the tower. I might even play the hunchback, with suitable make-up, though the way the Chap is going he might be more suitable without any. Whichever film I did I had learned a great deal from my first effort, especially about the dangers of operating on a bootlace. Or should that be a shoestring?

My only regret concerning my Western was falling out with the Chap over finance because money should never be the cause of friction between a dog and her man. Greed for money has been notorious down the ages for upsetting human relationships, even between sincerely loving people as close as brothers and sisters and parents and their children. It should never sully the human–canine relationship which operates on a higher plane remote from avarice. I was feeling so badly about our altercation that I was glad when I shook myself, even if it was to the anticlimax of seeing the deserted and clinically clean square outside the house.

145

CHAPTER 17
The Antiques Load Show

One of the most parroted in-words of the 1990s is 'culture'. It seems that every human race or sect has a culture – a conglomeration of customs, habits and beliefs – for which we should all be deeply grateful because it will enrich our own lives. However objectionable indigenous people may find some aspects of an alien culture, it is politically incorrect to criticise it. On the contrary, the more cultures to which we are subjected the more enriched will we all eventually be. Whether this is true or not must surely depend on the culture. I don't think that cannibals would enrich us much, for instance. However, I can think of one culture which has universally enriched the human species throughout recorded time: the canine culture. Believing that this unparalleled service has still not been sufficiently appreciated, I fell to wondering what I could do in that respect and hit upon a brilliant idea. I would promote the foundation of a National Museum of the Dog dedicated to the infinite aspects of our culture and the rich heritage (another in-word) with which we have endowed you. Furthermore, I would get the Millennium Commission to finance it or, failing that, the National Lottery.

All good ideas arise from experiences, and what generated that one was my habit of visiting so many antiques fairs and car boot sales with the Chap, who is an avid collector of bygones which are so often hyped up as 'museum pieces'. But before I could begin to raise the millions for a museum, for which honour the major cities would no doubt compete, I would need to do some groundwork if only to ensure that enough artefacts exist to fill it. I decided to begin my campaign by promoting the collection of canine memorabilia, with occasional sales devoted to them, as they do with cricket, golf and fishing. And what better hype for my project could there be than a programme of *The Antiques Road Show* on television devoted entirely to the canine culture?

At first I had problems convincing the producers that such an event would be viable and make good watching, but I am nothing if not persuasive. I pointed out, with all the force that I could muster, that to deny dogdom this chance would be to practise species discrimination and, being politically correct, as most of those in the BBC are these days, they eventually agreed. My other ace card – that seven million dog lovers is a not inconsiderable basic audience – also carried weight. Inevitably, there was concern about the possibility of dog fights but I assured them that there are none at Cruft's, where there are many more dogs competing in circumstances likely to generate jealousy and anger. The old showbiz chestnut about the professional danger of appearing with animals was quickly shown to be a load of old dogswallop by pointing out that, even with a name like Cattenborough, fame, fortune and a title can be achieved that way.

In discussions with the programme's anchor man, Hugh Scullery, whose name reminded me of places where I have been surreptitiously slipped many a tasty scrap, we had some difficulty in deciding on the venue. The district of Marylebone had something going for it but we finally settled for Barking Town Hall which, he agreed, had appropriate overtones. Fortunately, we were blessed with a fine day for the event and dogs of all breeds and social levels, their owners and other people from all over London and the home counties were queueing from early morning. The local buskers made the most of the opportunity, entertaining them with relevant songs like 'Get a long little doggy', which I have always assumed was dedicated to the dachshund or, perhaps, the basset hound.

When Mr Scullery introduced the programme he explained how the antiques timescale had been modified to suit the sadly brief canine lifespan. While the arbitrary minimum age of fifty years can qualify an item as 'antique' in human terms, this needs to be divided by seven or so on the canine scale, though objects substantially older than seven years would obviously be preferable. Mr Scullery was kind enough to mention my part in the show, explaining that I would be on hand throughout to assist with all canine aspects. Then, when the doors were opened there was the most extraordinary sight as the exhibitors trooped in with their treasured possessions.

There were dog bowls of every shape and size in pot, metal and plastic. There were dog baskets and dog beds of all descriptions, some beautifully upholstered and expensively covered. Some dogs were dragging old beanbags actually filled with dried beans, which must have been tempting the fates, plastic beans having not then been invented. There were armchairs and settees on which dogs were permitted to sleep. Some spoiled-rotten dogs arrived with the real beds on which they were allowed to lie all night. Two mastiffs were even pushing an old four-poster on squeaky castors. As I remarked to Mr Scullery, there was no doubt about the main preoccupations of most dogs – food and sleep! A few dogs were in harness pulling dog-carts and there was even a husky pulling an old sledge, but most were clutching precious possessions still concealed in cardboard boxes or wrapped in newspaper.

The first expert to fall to the camera's attention was the furniture specialist John Fly, who was examining an enormous, polished wooden kennel brought in by two Great Danes, father and son.

'This is a lovely piece of furniture, though perhaps I should say architecture, as it is clearly a dog-house,' Mr Fly began in his urbane manner. 'It has its original hinges and nails but I'm just slightly suspicious about it. There's something that's not quite right.' The Great Danes looked at each other with some apprehension. 'There is an infallible way of testing what I have in mind and that is to look inside.'

He then produced a torch and we pushed the lens of the camera in through the entrance of the kennel.

'There! Just as I thought. See what it says on the left-hand side – "Fyffe's Bananas". So I think we can say, definitely, that this kennel was made in this century and is probably not more than fifty years old, which is a good age in dog terms. Many thanks for bringing it in.'

The Great Danes, a breed apt to look a bit mournful at any time, were greatly disappointed and not entirely convinced, I thought, as the cameras panned away from them to a table nearby.

There, surrounded by a crowd of dogs and their owners, was the ever-smiling ceramics expert Henry Sandman, who I think is aptly named because he is such a kindly soul that he is just like my idea of the fairy-tale character who sends puppies and babies to sleep. He was examining a brown, pot bowl which had been brought in by an Old English sheepdog.

'It's round and probably used for a dog's food or water because it has DOG in large black letters on the side,' he said. 'Of course, we cannot be absolutely sure of that because it may have been used for a cat, in spite of the name on it, but the odds are that it was for a dog.'

The Old English sheepdog looked surprised which probably indicated that, with all that wool permanently pulled over its eyes, it had never seen the lettering before.

'There's no maker's mark on it but I notice the price there,' Mr Sandman said, pointing to a faint mark with his finger. '"One shilling and sixpence", which definitely dates it before the introduction of decimal coinage. I'm afraid that's probably still too late for art deco, which would greatly have increased its value, because it's so much in fashion, but we can definitely call it art dogo.'

The sheepdog's face, or what could be seen of it, lit up. Good old Henry, I thought. Always so anxious that nobody should go away disappointed.

'As to value,' Mr Sandman went on, rubbing his chin, 'I should say that if it came up at auction it might bring fifty pence.' Then, sensing the let-down, he added, hastily, 'That's ten shillings in old money, you know. So, not a bad investment, really. What's next?'

The answer came in the form of another dog bowl looking exactly like the first but marked FIDO. Mr Sandman's face lit up immediately.

'Now this is of an earlier period and has to be Victorian! Fido, which means faithful, was a common name for a dog in Victorian times but then it went completely out of fashion. Is there a dog in the room called Fido?'

From that vast canine throng there was no answer. Come to that, I've never heard of another dog called Dido, either.

'Unfortunately there is a crack in it and it has been repaired, which greatly reduces its value. Now, if it had been perfect . . .'

If any of us had been perfect! I thought.

'You must have had some splendid meals out of it,' Mr Sandman said to the bull terrier who had brought the bowl in. 'I'm sure it has great sentimental value for you. Keep it in the family! Pass it on to your pups!'

Mr Sandman had better luck with a Spode dish used by a ludicrously spoiled lap-dog, some Meissen pugs, a pair of Rocking'em poodles and some other china dogs brought in by owners. It is odd how you call them all china even if they are made in another country, which is very confusing for a dog but, then, your language is full of such oddities. With us a bark is a bark is a bark.

The metal bowls were the province of David Scatty, who was whirling one expertly in his hands as the camera was wheeled towards him.

'Well, I can tell you that this one is definitely Chinese,' he said to the whippet who had brought it.

'How do you know that?' the whippet asked.

'It says "Made in Hong Kong" on the bottom.'

'Ah, I hadn't noticed that,' said the whippet, who was not only disappointed but looked foolish.

'Do you know the provenance?' Mr Scatty asked but the whippet, who no doubt was brilliant at winning races, obviously had no idea what he meant.

'Is that the name of an insurance company?' he asked.

'Not to worry,' Mr Scatty said with a nice smile as he handed the bowl back. 'Keep it long enough and it will become collectable.'

There was an enormous heap of bowls on Mr Scatty's table and he picked up a huge one belonging to a wolfhound. I have often wondered what would happen if one of the experts chanced to drop a valuable object which they never seem to do, at least on camera. In the case of any of the metal bowls, however, it would not have mattered much as most of them were already dented, mainly, I suspect, by the dogs pushing the bowls around when they were empty to create a din, hopefully indicating that they were still hungry, a dodge which I have found never works.

Meanwhile, Mr Scullery and I were having a great game matching dogs to owners, the women owners of Pekes being the easiest to spot. There is a theory that owners grow to look like their dogs but I suspect the truth is that they acquire dogs which look like them. Fat people choose big dogs who become fatter and develop jowls because the whole household eats too much while skinny breeds chosen by thin people are likely to stay slim. Whiskery men seem to prefer long-haired dogs and so on. I found the owners' dress equally revealing. Many of the ladies had clearly bothered to go to the hairdresser in case they might appear on camera, but most of the men just wore their casual multi-coloured shirts, trousers and trainers – old rams dressed up as lamb, I thought, in the case of the older ones.

One table bore several objects which, from the reaction of the watchers, both human and canine, produced mixed feelings. They were stuffed dogs, some in glass cases but most just mounted on a wooden board. The most life-like was a Peke which was curled up on a little upholstered stool, looking very alive. Another one was a famous greyhound in full stretch and there was a stuffed bulldog with a Union Jack sewn on its breast and looking remarkably like Winston Churchill. As I looked at them with some distaste I realised that it was one way of staying in the pack after demise and something of an honour, I suppose, but, in that case, why aren't humans stuffed occasionally? Looking round the crowd I saw that, as with some of the dogs, some people would stuff better than others while several in the hall looked stuffed already. There is, of course, a common expression 'get stuffed!' which has always rather baffled me, but the Chap says that its origin is associated with the reverse of dying. Anyway, since most of the stuffed dogs which were not in glass cases looked distinctly flyblown and were losing sawdust, I decided that I would prefer not to be and made a note to say so in my will.

We stopped the camera by the table reserved for treen which, I understand, is the collective name for things made of wood, just in time to see the expert lift the cork from the little wooden brandy-barrel brought in by a St Bernard and hear him mutter 'Dear God! What I could do to a drink!'

Then it was back to John Fly, who was examining a much smaller kennel belonging to a cocker spaniel and was so beautifully constructed that it was clearly an indoor piece from some stately home. He slid his hand, lovingly, over the rich veneer with a cry of 'Ouch!' as it picked up a long splinter, but in true professional fashion, since the show must always go on, he proceeded to apply the Fyffe's Bananas test. Naturally, the entrance to this kennel was very small and once Mr Fly had got his head through it he found that he could not get it out. There was a muffled cry of

'Keep those damned cameras away!' but it was too late. In fact, I made sure that they got them there. Not that I don't like Mr Fly. On the contrary, I do, very much, but I think that dogs should never miss any chance to cut humans down to size, and the more famous and more dignified the better.

Eventually his head was safely extracted and as the piece had passed the bananas test, and others which he did not mention, he pronounced it genuine Georgian, but only George the Sixth.

'You've got some woodworm in there,' he said to the cocker spaniel, dusting down the lapels of his smart dark suit. 'It's still active and you should get it treated without delay.'

On hearing this I noticed that one old man took off smartly, limping slightly. I deduced that he had a wooden leg which he was anxious to preserve.

A tremendous argument among several experts ensued over a strange metal object which looked like some kind of trap and was alleged by its human owner to be a canine chastity belt for the rear end of a smallish dog. It was quickly agreed that it was too small for a woman and men didn't have them. It was certainly old but the little padlock with which it had once been fitted and by which it might have been dated was missing. Clearly it had been designed and made by men who would not have dreamed of making a chastity belt for a male dog, any more than for themselves, but I strongly suspected that it was really a muzzle for the front end of a large dog. However, the more interesting interpretation prevailed and they decided that it was a museum piece and too rare and unusual to be valued.

The nice lady who dealt with toys had a wide choice of old teddy bears with chewed-off ears, golliwogs and specimens of Paddington dog in various stages of decline. There were balls of all shapes and sizes, mostly punctured except for the oldest which were made of wood, imprinted with the teeth of dogs long since dead. The lady's most frequent remark to cover her embarrassingly minuscule estimates at auction was 'What a pity this is not in its original box. It makes such a difference to the value.'

The table for dog collars was one of the best attended as so many had been submitted for estimate. There were very wide collars with sharp spikes said to have belonged to medieval dogs of war, and some were inscribed with remarks like 'If you can read this you are pushing your luck' and 'I am Joe Bloggs bitch. Whose son of a bitch are you?' The collar creating greatest interest was a small one encrusted with diamonds and made for some film star's miniature poodle by Tiffany's. I had little doubt that its cost had been set against tax as essential PR since it had been the subject of so many photographs of the star in question nursing her dog. Since some of the collars were alleged to have been worn by dogs belonging to famous men I made a note to secure one of the Chap's collars for my projected museum, where it would feature in a section of collars worn by the owners of famous dogs.

There were some quite appalling, long, heavy chains used in the past (and, I suspect, even in the present) to anchor guard dogs to stakes. The one causing most interest was a slip chain from a bloodhound used by the warders at Dartmoor for recapturing dangerous criminals, the morbid human interest in crime being a surefire draw.

Inevitably, there was a collection of poop-scoopers which, with my earthy sense of humour, I would have consigned to the Pong period. While it is only recently that what one might call designer poop-scoopers have become available, various other tools, such as small shovels, have been reserved for that purpose and several of these were on display. One excessively hopeful Dobermann had brought in what he claimed to be an Iron Age poop-scooper which he had found buried in a garden. Various experts examined it and, while none was prepared to commit himself, I sensed that they all believed that it was just an old garden trowel that had lost its handle but they did not want to offend the Dobermann, which looked a tough customer, or its beer-bellied owner who looked even tougher and was clearly smelling money.

As the animal most commonly depicted in Man's best pictures is Man's best friend, the area dealing with art was stacked with paintings, prints and a few tapestries. There was repeated mention of famous artists whose names sounded to me like Canineletto, Guardog, Whatho, Van Duck, Jan van Egg and Dogarth. I was surprised to see none by Whistler, who should have been good at communicating with dogs.

The weight of what could only be called bric-à-brac was a record for any of the road shows. There were grooming brushes without many bristles, combs without many teeth, lockets containing wisps of dog hair, cigarette cards about dogs in series of fifty, dog money-boxes and roasting spits which had been worked by a dog running on a wheel. One fox terrier had managed to bring in a sizeable collection of old gramophone records, all with labels showing that rather plain-looking member of his breed listening to his master's voice. I had always thought they would have sold even more with a Labrador. There was a dog's artificial leg, alleged to have been made by a sailor on Nelson's flagship, and a fossil leg-bone of a Neanderthal dog, which the archaeologists had called Roger because it was lodged in the clay. There were even old tins which had contained dog food and enamelled advertisements for dog biscuits.

It was, of course, the owners who had collected this astonishing array. A dog's need for possessions is very modest and it is only in the human species that the collecting instinct exists, if that is what it is. While a prudent dog might stockpile a few bones the mania to collect things – almost any things – is peculiarly human. Apes don't have it and, with the exception of a few birds like magpies and jackdaws which like bright objects, I do not know of any other creatures that do.

With everything I experience, and with the dog–man relationship ever in mind, I try to learn a little more about how the human mind ticks and I concluded, from what I had seen that day and previously, that only the human mind is acquisitive, by which I mean takes pleasure out of the sheer possession of things. It must be in the genes because small boys have it and with many people it becomes almost a mania. Why? It cannot simply be an expression of the hunting instinct because, in that case, I should have it and I don't. Though most people do not collect objects with the prime purpose of eventually making money out of them the habit seems to be a form of greed because collectors nearly always want more and go to great lengths to get them. With some rich ones this can become such a compulsion that they will order pictures to be stolen so that they can gloat over them in private.

My own theory to explain this is that it all began with living in caves which men felt they needed to liven up with furniture and ornaments because moving them about and cleaning them gave their women something to do and kept them out of mischief when the men were away hunting. This was exacerbated by the invention of the skin bag and the wheel which made it easier for men to bring things back after raids on other tribes. Then, when possessions became a sign of superiority, both the men and their women began to compete with other families to see who could get the most. The habit has burgeoned ever since with the accent more and more on old and rare things, though some men collect items as new as the numbers on railway engines! It is difficult for a dog to understand why anything which is old and worn should become more valuable than something which is spanking new, especially when this seems to apply only to inanimate objects. So far as old people and old dogs are concerned the respect and value allotted to them seems to decline the older they get, at least in the Western culture.

The prices now paid for very old objects defy all sensible explanation, with seven million pounds being paid at auction for a slab of an old stone carving which had resided for years on a school tuck-shop wall, and far more being paid for old canvases covered with paint 400 years ago, which may seem a long time but is only five human lifespans. What seems even crazier to a dogjective observer is that antiques are subject to fashion, almost like women's clothes. Furniture, paintings and ceramics which attracted big prices a few years ago may suddenly slump in value, though their nature has not changed at all except that they have got even older which, one would imagine, should increase their worth. My experience on *The Antiques Road Show* did little to make any dog sense out of this strange human foible.

My associate, Mr Scullery, brought the proceedings at Barking Town Hall to a close with a guessing game. He showed an antique piece on the

153

screen with a nice prize in pet-food vouchers for any dog who could answer a question about an old Toby jug in the form of a begging dog. The clue was that it involved a king who is not remembered for much else but small court dogs and large courtesans. I knew that the answer had to be a Charles II spaniel because we have a jug like that but, being involved with the programme, I couldn't compete, which was a pity. Summing up, Mr Scullery, with me by his side, said it was one of the best days they had experienced and that, save for the odd skirmish, all the dogs had come through with flying collars. He then gave a nice puff for my museum idea with an address to which contributions should be sent.

All in all, on returning to reality, it had been one of my more pleasant reveries and I had learned a lesson which I suppose we should all put into practice: never throw anything away because today's rubbish may be tomorrow's antiques. The potential money that must be dumped each week in wheelie-bins!

CHAPTER 18

Dido Queen of Scots

On the night before we were due to travel north for the spring salmon fishing in 1994 I had come on heat which, of course, was no fault of mine. The Chap had been given advanced warning because my most persistent and faithful admirer, the wandering Jack Russell and village troubadour called Charlie whom I have mentioned before, had somehow got wind of my condition. The Chap says that Charlie must have a calendar, which is not impossible because if dogs have a built-in biological clock which enables us to tell the time of day, especially feeding time, why shouldn't we have a built-in calendar? Anyway, however Charlie does it, he had begun to lie in wait outside the back gates from which I usually emerge when taken for a walk. He sits there for so long hoping for a sight of me, even when I am not on heat, that he reminds the Boss of that song in *My Fair Lady* about a lover being delirious just to be in the street where the girl of his dreams lives, though in Charlie's case it would be *My Dark Bitch*. So it is not surprising that he often figures in my fantasies. Aggravating though he sometimes is, I admire persistence and loyalty.

Frankly, I enjoy feeling sexy but because of the domestic problems we would face when staying with our friends in Northumberland, on our way north, and then in Scotland, the Chap and the vet decided that it would be better for everyone, including me, if my season was suppressed with an injection. My opinion wasn't asked but the deed was duly done and, in the event, I was glad because it meant that I could mooch about the banks of the Tay at will with no fears of attention from the ghillies' dogs, especially one called Teal, who is exceptionally well endowed.

There was no fishing on the Sunday, when we arrived, because salmon may not be pursued on the sabbath in Scotland, though trout can be, which makes me wonder which fish is being discriminated against. So we broke our journey to visit the ancient Palace of Scone (pronounced Scoon), on the edge of Perth.

The trouble with visiting any historic place in Scotland is that it is so difficult to separate the real events from the legends. This is true of England too: Merrie England is loaded with fiction just like Bonny Scotland, but not to the same extent because so much of Scotland's history was deliberately invented by one man – the aptly named Sir Walter Scottie. It was Scottie, after whom the sparky little dog must be named, who made Scotland such a romantic place, meaning that the stories about it are remote from reality but much more exciting, though Shakespeare made his contribution with *Macbeth*. We dogs never cease to be astonished by the extent to which you humans love to delude yourselves. Even in your intimate relationships you prefer fantasised versions of life to reality, calling them 'romantic'. I am now so humanised myself that I enjoy delusion as much as you do, a luxury a dog could never have afforded in the wild, where stark reality rules. In particular, I love the Scottish myths as much as any other visitor. The atmosphere they have created (for which Scottish tourism should be ever grateful) makes me wish I had some Scottish blood. I do have a slight Scottish connection because my forebears came from Newfoundland, an island off the coast of Labrador where there was immigrant Scottish blood among the settlers who were responsible for creating my breed. So I sport a tartan collar in Scotland and I would like to go the whole hog and wear a kilt but it would not hang properly.

Scone Palace proved to be rather different from most of the other sites we had visited such as Glamis Castle, for instance, where Macbeth never lived, for there is no doubt that it really was at Scone that the ancient Scottish kings and queens were crowned. It turned out to be extra special for me because in one of the rooms there is a painting by Zoffany of a pretty, chocolate-coloured lady called Dido, the daughter of a housekeeper who had been freed from slavery and treated like one of the family, as is right and proper for anyone with that noble name or of that distinguished colour.

When the Chap, the Boss and I were going round the Palace grounds we visited the Moot Hill, the little mound where the Scottish monarchs used to be crowned sitting on a small slab of rock called the Stone of Scone. The English King Edward the First nicked the stone and put it in Westminster Abbey where it resides under the old Coronation Chair, so that English kings and queens (who are also now kings and queens of the Scots) are crowned on it though they don't have to sit on its cold, hard surface as the tougher Scots did. I know how uncomfortable it was because there is a replica of the old stone on the Moot Hill and the Chap could not resist photographing me sitting on it in queenly fashion.

Through all my fan mail I know that to many I am already a Queen of

Hearts, a title currently coveted by someone else of note, but to imagine oneself as a real queen is a vanity that appeals to every female, even though the job would probably be dreadful. So, as I identify not just with Dido, the great Queen of Carthage, but with other famous female rulers, who else could I fantasise about after that experience at Scone but Mary Queen of Scots? Note that she was never called Mary Queen of Scotland which, I understand, is because she never owned the land which was always regarded as belonging to the clans. (Incidentally, my clan happens to be Stuart, like hers. Why? Between you and me, solely because I liked the colour of the tartan. 'Just like a woman!' as the Chap says.)

I already knew about Mary Queen of Scots because the Chap always bangs on about her raunchy affair with the Earl of Bothwell every time we fill up with fuel at the M74 Bothwell services on the way back from salmon fishing. Apparently, after the Earl of Bothwell had blown up Mary's husband, Darnley, she took off and married him, scandalising the Scottish gentry. One day we even visited Bothwell Castle where Sir Walter Scottie wrote his famous poem 'Young Lochinvar'. What made me identify with Mary was that she was a *femme fatale* if ever there was one and I have always fancied myself as a *chienne fatale*, a fateful, if not fatal, bitch, especially as on the day we visited Scone the natural urge of my heat had not been entirely eliminated by the vet's injection and I was still feeling randy.

It was therefore, inevitable, seeing the way that I am made, that when we arrived at Balmacneil, the lovely house on the Tay near Dunkeld where we were to stay for the week with our friend, Connie Ward, I should fall to thinking about Mary. The conditions were perfect. The sun was shining and I was able to settle down on the lawn with a bone which I had regally liberated from Connie's chocolate Labrador pup Amber, just as the English had requisitioned the Stone of Scone. I was being held captive in a castle on an island in the middle of a loch and I realised who I was from the beautiful white ruff round my neck. Once, when visiting the vet, he decked me out, just for fun, with one of those wide white plastic collars which are used to stop a dog scratching a wound on its face. I was told that I looked rather fetching in it but this ruff was something much more becoming, as I admired myself in the dark old mirror by candlelight in my gloomy chamber. I also saw that I was wearing a rather fetching head-dress and some pearls so I had no doubt who I was. A darker version, admittedly, but Mary Queen of Scots without doubt. She too, from all accounts, had been well-proportioned with a lively personality, bewitching charm and dignity of bearing, as I have often been described. She had a large nose but, then, so have I and it can be a mark of character. 'Every inch a queen,' I thought as I continued to gaze in the mirror though, being nearly six feet tall, Mary had more inches than me. Still not a bad likeness, but what was the point of looking so attractive when I was locked up in this grim, stone-walled chamber in the turret of an isolated castle? Most days the only male I saw was my gaoler when he brought in my food which was comprehensively awful. I was so sick of the oat cuisine that I fully understood why prison régime is called porridge. And me used to the best French cooking as the widow of the King of France! For some reason I have never yet fathomed the Scots eat porridge standing up, saying that it's a tradition. Perhaps when they started eating it they had no chairs but then, apart from bones, I eat everything standing up and drink that way too.

I was also in great danger because all sorts of people were plotting to make me Queen of England. I don't mind opening a few fairs and fêtes – *noblesse oblige* and all that stuff – but to do it almost every day and to have to smile and be polite all the time without ever looking bored would, I confess, be beyond me. As for power, I do like that but I wield as much as I want already. Still, I suppose it must all be worth it just to be called 'Your Majesty' because few ever want to give it up.

That was what I was – 'Her Majesty' – and I would have been happy to open anything just to get out of that locked chamber. There was a window but it opened on to the dark, rippling water of the loch. All I could do was to wait for some Dog Roy or Young Doginvar to come out of the West. What a hope! Then, just when I was thinking that all I had to look forward to was yet another bowl of lumpy porridge in the morning, there was a tap on the lead-lined window pane. I picked up a candlestick and peered out. There, in the bright moonlight, was my faithful friend Charlie, the Jack Russell, dressed as the Bonnie Prince and dangling on a rope. (I know that the dates for Mary and Bonnie Prince Charlie don't tally, but if Scottie could rewrite history why shouldn't I?)

As Charlie heaved himself through the casement into the room, wearing his bright red Stuart tartan bonnet and kilt, his claymore got stuck in the window-frame so that he fell in with a crash, which was not surprising as the claymore was longer than he was. Fortunately the guard outside the door was asleep, as usual, and after a brief embrace Charlie announced that he had come to rescue me and take me to England where we could sort out, between us, who should eventually rule there as well as in Scotland since, by birth, both of us were entitled to the lot. Privately, having taken a close look at my own real-life offspring, I have always felt that settling the succession by heredity has to be crazy, but this was no time to argue. Seeing black-and-white Charlie in that extraordinary rig-out gave me the giggles but I did my best to suppress them as, with a low, sweeping bow and holding his bonnet in his right paw, he motioned me to slide down the rope into a boat waiting below. I wish he had told me that there was a big knot in the middle of the rope. He had obviously forgotten it himself because he let out a dreadful howl as he followed me down. The knot was unpleasant enough for me but, obviously, it held dual hazards for a male.

Taking the oars, he insisted on rowing round to the entrance to the castle where he opened his sporran and took out a big tube of superglue. After squirting it all into the keyhole to jam the mechanism, he raised his right paw in a rude gesture and muttered 'Up yours, Moray,' referring to the leader of the Protestant nobles who had locked me up. Then he cocked his leg against the heavy oak front door providing proof – which, personally, I did not need after my affair with the Earl of Bothwell – that Scotsmen wear nothing under their kilts, but there was more to it than that.

'I wanted to leave my mark – "Charlie was here!"' he whispered in a hoarse Scottish accent. 'My mark is all over Scotland and it'll soon be all over England.'

Withdrawing his claymore from its scabbard he raised it in a further gesture of defiance in front of the castle. 'We will return!' he said, as loudly as he dared and rolling his rs, like Scotsmen do. As he tried to sheath it with his short arms he cut one of his paws, not badly but enough to draw blood which I saw was not blue but, like mine, the same colour as anybody else's, though of course we had to continue to pretend it was blue, in which sense all we royals are pretenders. Then, as he prepared to clamber back into the boat, he went an awful purler over his claymore again. (Why is it impossible not to laugh when this sort of thing happens?) I found it hard to resist telling him that his claymore was far too long for his body but felt that it would be unhelpful and might offend him. Besides, we needed to be away without any further melodramatic delays.

As he rowed Charlie started to sing, softly at first, 'Speed bonny boat like a bird on the wing!' and as I looked at this sparse, rather ludicrous 'Young Pretender', who in real life is of pensionable age, I thought, 'You'll never make the throne of England or anywhere else', an assessment which was strengthened almost immediately for we had not gone far when he rowed right into a rock and the boat was more like a floundering duck than a bird on the wing as it filled with cold loch water. There was nothing to do but swim for it and we dog-paddled hopefully towards land with his claymore causing further difficulty and threatening to drag him down. At that moment Charlie was certainly not my darling.

I was not afraid because I was too occupied thinking about my lovely ruff which had taken hours to starch and iron that morning – by one of my bitches-in-waiting, of course – though I did manage to keep my head-dress dry, a trick I had learned in real life from the Boss who, when nearly drowning once in the Tay, still managed to keep her hair do from getting wet.

'You stupid dog,' I spluttered, as regally as I could in the circumstances, wondering if the Bonnie Prince's boatmanship was the historic origin of the immortal phrase 'A proper Charlie!'

On reaching the shore we shook ourselves dryish, as only dogs can, and giving one last look at the castle we could see lights and the noise of boats being launched in pursuit. It wasn't just me they were after but Charlie too. Two royal Stuarts for the price of one!

'To the border!' cried Charlie, drawing his sword yet again and striking another dramatic pose. 'Me to rouse the clans and march on London at the head of a thousand dogs. You to seek sanctuary with your cousin Elizabeth.'

Not a bad idea, I thought. Queen Elizabeth was not only kind to her corgis but liked her Labrador gundogs even more. So I should be blown in with her. The annoying thing was that being so much bigger and better built than Charlie I could run faster than he could and repeatedly had to wait for him. Furthermore, he kept stopping to cock his leg in spite of my pleas that the last thing we wanted anyone who might be following us to know was that Charlie had been there.

However, in no time, as can happen in reveries, we saw the signpost to Gretna Green where Charlie, having anointed it, suggested a romantic stop-over at the blacksmith's where we might get fed as well as married – an incestuous proposition but that, I am told, often happens in human fantasies. The blacksmith was a huge hairy man with an even hairier, obscene sporran. He must have recognised one of us, or both – he could hardly fail to spot Charlie and I suppose I should have thrown my ruff away and buried my pearls but, then, how would Queen Elizabeth know who I was when I reached her? Anyway, the blacksmith probably thought he was in for a big reward or ransom for he immediately threatened us with his hammer and ordered us to put up our paws and surrender. Of course, our response was to do or die. Charlie's courage has never been in doubt, in spite of his small size, for he attacks any other dog who pays any attention to me when he's around, however big or ferocious. And they usually concede.

The gallant Charlie cocked his leg on the blacksmith's and drew his claymore with a flourish. Abandoning any pretence at majesty, I bit the blacksmith on the other leg, being careful to avoid the one which Charlie had just patronised. Then, just as the hateful traitor was about to bring his hammer down on Charlie's head, I awoke with a start. What I had really bitten into was the bone belonging to Amber, the resident pup, and, having just reappeared from her siesta, she didn't like it and was letting me know.

Ah well, so much for being a queen! It is too full of uncertainty for my taste. I'll settle for being a commoner which, perhaps, is what any real queen dreams about.

On my return home to Kintbury I was gratified to see Charlie still sitting outside the back gate where, we were told, he had been most of the week when I had been missing. Ah! Normally, the Chap would have left Charlie outside but this time he invited him into the garden to keep me company, feeling sorry for him and also thinking that I must be missing Amber's company, which indeed I was. So what happened? Charlie had one sniff of my rear end, decided that he was too late, cocked his leg on the plum tree and asked to be let out. Dogs!

So much for the gallant Bonnie Prince Charlie! So much for being a *chienne fatale*! Ah well! Fantasy is almost always more rewarding than reality. Sad, isn't it? Yet, without its leavening and the pleasure, excitement and laughs it provides, life might be too stark for some us – maybe all of us.

CHAPTER 19

The Barker Prize for Literature

By now, you will have appreciated that I have experienced some pretty savage daymares at the hands of men, and a few at the paws of dogs, but none has been so excoriating as that inflicted by that canine anathema – a cat! What happened in my reverie was that this book, *Life's a Bitch!*, was nominated for the Barker Prize which had been sponsored by a petfood manufacturer and was being run by the Kennel Club. My book had been shortlisted for the prize, along with five others in the genre, after being glowingly serialised by a national newspaper with widespread publicity on television. The prize, a year's supply of tinned pet food, meant nothing to me because I would get that anyway, but the Chap, who is of canny Yorkshire origins, viewed the saving with some anticipation. The main reward however, as with the Booker Prize for human authors, was in the increased sales which could be expected in the bookshops. Again the Chap had a pecuniary interest through his access to my royalties because my account with Lloyds Bank has to be joint with him to make it legal.

Three of my rivals posed little threat, in my view. Two of them were Cavalier King Charles spaniels, one of whom had authored a small, slim collection of letters while the other's effort was an even smaller and slimmer volume of poems. The third rival, a pit-bull terrier called Adolf recently deceased at the hands of the police because he had savaged three people, one of whom happened to be a magistrate, was perhaps a more serious contender. His book, *My Fight for Life*, was a tear-jerking account of his incarceration and legal battles following the panic legislation about dangerous fighting dogs which his owner, a skin-headed bruiser, had refused to obey. It was already selling like hot biscuits among the neo-Nazis in Germany under the title *Mein Kampf ums Leben*. For that reason alone he stood little chance with the Barker Prize judges who, inevitably, were left-wing, avant-garde and opposed to violence except in support of their own peculiar causes such as the shipment of live calves to the Continent. The fourth entry was just an English version of the book by Millie, the spaniel who had been First Bitch in the White House during the presidential days of George and Barbara Bush. Her book, ghosted by the First Lady, had been a real money-spinner, earning far more in one year than the President's salary and outselling the memoirs of the previous leader Ronald Reagan, far more Americans being interested in the First Bitch than in the last President. However, much as I like Millie with whom I have been in touch, her book was little more than a collection of colour photographs with captions.

From what I had heard, the judges, among whom there had already been some fierce back-biting, were a motley, prejudiced lot likely to favour any mongrel peddling a hard-luck story. Recently, far too much attention has been paid to underdogs, both canine and human, so I was relieved to learn that all we finalists were upperdogs, being thoroughbreds, apart from the pit-bull, who wasn't there. Then, to my horror and disgust, the sixth shortlisted book turned out to be by a cat, and an undercat at that! Called *Catty Come Home!* it was just what I had feared – a depressing tale about a homeless and generally disadvantaged, three-legged, lesbian tabby with a drink problem caused by licking the dregs of discarded beer cans. Most of the book consisted of the tabby's private thoughts as it lay in its cardboard box underneath some arch or other in – yes, you guessed it – Catford. After being raped – what stray female cat isn't, gay or not? – it was pregnant again, giving it the opportunity to bang on about the unfairness of being a single parent who had been allowed to fall through the safety net and was being let down by the system. 'I blame the government' was on almost every page.

Really, if someone wants to create a Miaow Prize that's up to them but the Barker Prize should be strictly reserved for dogs like the Booker Prize is restricted to humans. Unfortunately the rules of entry did not specify dogs any more than, I imagine, the rules of the Booker Prize specify humans, because it was regarded as unnecessary. No doubt the owner of the cat which purported to have written *Catty Come Home!* had consulted some sharp lawyer and the Kennel Club, which is accused of so much, had decided to avoid being accused of racial prejudice. So we were stuck with this wretched cat and her rotten little 'social document'. On sheer merit I did not fear it, but there was no accounting for the vagaries of the judges who were all likely to be politically correct and in favour of positive discrimination.

I was cheered up to learn that the announcement of the award and the ceremony of its presentation were not to be held at the Dogchester but at Grrrosvenor House, then the flagship hotel of Lord Forte who is not only a proven doggy person but an old friend and admirer of mine. Furthermore, there used to be quite a few Forte shares in our joint portfolio. Naturally, I had long discussions with the Boss about what to wear for the dressy occasion and we settled for an unusual evening collar with red studs, lit by a little battery. The Chap, who would be with me on the podium, decided on his chocolate velvet jacket and matching bow-tie, which I found rather touching.

The two Cavaliers, who clearly knew each other, had cute little top-knots tied with ribbon, as did their lady owners who looked rather twee, I thought. The owner of the pit-bull, who it later transpired was a nightclub bouncer with convictions for assault, was in a hired suit that didn't fit him. He stood there, looking as pathetic as possible, holding his late dog's lead, a thick steel chain attached to a huge empty collar equipped with spikes an inch long. The purported author of *Catty Come Home!* turned out to be a large female Persian which, I suppose, should now be called Iranian. With almost bouffant fur making her head seem outsize and a distinctly superior gaze she was described by the Chap as 'a feline Barbara Cartland', though blue rather than pink. She was so shampooed and perfumed that I doubt she could have done any research in the back streets of Catford and looked as though she dictated everything while lying, full-length, on a pumped-up satin cushion in Mayfair. Anyway, there we were – four dogs, the ghost of a dead one, and this moggie.

All our ghost-writers, the Chap in my case, were photographed holding up the six books. Whenever the television cameras were in action the pit-bull man managed to rattle his chain and empty collar in transparent attempts to curry sympathy from the audience.

The judgement went just as I had expected. It was already clear that the cat book had won when the chairperson of the judges, a stringy authoress of stream-of-consciousness novels, began to enthuse about the 'profound social implications' of *Catty Come Home!* Calling it a cry for help for the camp cat community, 'a grossly underprivileged mini-minority to which society had paid a degree of attention that was totally unacceptable – all the clichés were there – she construed it as an inspired message for human society concerning the homeless of all species, especially those who were confused about their sexuality, as I suspect the lady was herself. Here was a pitiable creature with which so many of us could identify, she claimed, though I was damned if I could. Catty had been dealt a cruel hand by a society which had failed her in every conceivable way, preventing her from realising her potential. Purely because of the government's determination to save money to cut taxes in time for the next general election, no effort whatever had been made to give Catty a bionic leg or even a wooden one which might have helped her achieve her aspirations. There were murmurs of agreement from some of the audience which was well peppered with people from the civil liberties industry.

I could see the two Cavaliers whispering to each other and with my acute hearing could detect what they said. Apparently they had discovered that four of the judges were flat-dwellers who owned cats. Neither the Cavaliers, the pit-bull terrier nor I had ever stood a dog-in-hell's chance.

When *Catty Come Home!* was finally declared the winner by a majority decision I managed to keep my cool under constant eye-to-eye contact with the Chap who, brassed off as he was, insisted that any Labrador, and especially a chocolate, must maintain its decorum in all circumstances, however provocative. For the two Cavaliers, however, the disappointment and resentment at being beaten by a mere cat were too much. They blew their top-knots, pulled their little leads away and the Persian cat, seeing them coming, leapt and clawed her way up the expensive brocade curtains behind the podium, knocking over a tray of glasses on the way. Thank God the pit-bull terrier wasn't there, though for a moment I thought his bereaved owner was about to join in, probably concentrating his energy on the judges.

As the Persian hissed defiance from the safety of the pelmet, it was easy to see, from their body language, that most of the audience seated at the dinner tables were pro-dog, though a few, mainly women, were rooting for the cat. Some of the men started laying bets on the outcome as the Cavaliers tugged at the curtain, with remarkable force for their size. I felt cowardly in not joining in because, with my substantial weight, we might have dragged the lot down, cat and all, but the Chap had me very firmly under control. I was very pleased that he had done so for, at that moment, in walked Lord Forte in his purposeful way, his moustache bristling in his determination to restore order, preserve his curtains and dismiss the offenders from his hotel. Had I been embroiled in the mêlée we might never have been asked to his Boxing Day shoot again, and neither the Chap nor the Boss would ever have forgiven me. Nor would I have forgiven myself.

The fearful prospect of such a disaster aroused me with a start, but like so many of my reveries this one had a creative spin-off: I would agitate for the establishment of a real-life Barker Prize restricted to dogs and with the award being treats which we would not otherwise get, not everyday petfood.

I know that the number of cats in Britain now slightly exceeds the number of dogs and is rising, mainly through their indiscriminate breeding, and that cat food has become a substantial market. But petfood manufacturers should appreciate on which side their cans are really weighted. There are still seven million of us and we eat far more than cats. Indeed, it is mainly because cats are cheaper to feed – apart from not needing to be taken for walks in this couch potato age – that so many people are giving them house room. With the recession receding, the adoration of the moggie may well be a passing fad so, on all counts, a Barker Prize should clearly have priority.

Those prepared to sponsor such awards for animal literature, which, I feel sure, is an expanding art form with enormous potential, could also profit from my fantasy. They should never forget the wisdom of the old patriotic poet who makes those exceedingly good cakes which I enjoy so much – 'Oh, Dog is Dog and Cat is Cat and never the twain should compete'.

Though it may be unwise to reveal my paw at this stage, I am already working on the opus which I shall submit to the judges – the libretto and lyrics for a rip-roaring musical called *Dogs!*

Epidog

In these few private feelings and fantasies, which are just a fraction of my fat portfolio of recorded meditations, I have barely scratched the surface of the oddities of human behaviour, but putting them on record has done wonders for my personal feel-good factor. It is a great joy to be a dog of achievement when so many of my species merit only the epitaph 'I came, I saw, I wuffed'.

I know that dogs who live in glasshouses shouldn't throw bones – I spend a lot of time in our conservatory and have quite a few quirks of my own – but seen through canine eyes and imagination, you must concede that you are a funny lot with some extraordinary habits and institutions. Speaking for all of my kind though, as I am confident that I can, we would not have you any other way.